Wolves in Sheep's Clothing
False Prophets in the Church

by

Thomas P. Hill
Master Productions
East Lansing, MI 48823

Copyright © 2009 by Thomas P. Hill

Wolves in Sheep's Clothing
by Thomas P. Hill

Printed in the United States of America

ISBN 978-1-60791-414-3

All rights reserved solely by the author. The author guarantees all contents are original and do not infringe upon the legal rights of any other person or work. No part of this book may be reproduced in any form without the permission of the author. The views expressed in this book are not necessarily those of the publisher.

Unless otherwise indicated, Bible quotations are taken from the King James Version of the Bible.

www.xulonpress.com

Acknowledgements

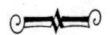

Someone once said that many hands make light work. This certainly describes the involvement of several dear ones who aided in the completion of this project. First, I thank my dear heavenly Father for impressing on me by His Spirit the gravity of this issue. I recognize His hand in the development of this work and the instruction and enablement of the Holy Spirit to complete it.

Second, I thank my wife, Diane, who struggled with me in prayer and counsel as I labored over these studies. She worked many long hours in revising my sometimes rough expressions to make them understandable.

Next, I thank our friends, Dr. Bill Brown, and his wife, Suzanne. They, too, spent many hours revising and suggesting corrections and improvements to these studies. More than one restaurant excursion involved the discussion of these manuscripts, including encouragement to press on. Sometimes they even paid for our meals ... what grace.

Finally, I thank the dear people who make up the Sunday Night Gatherings where I first delivered these thoughts. They, too, provided encouragement to seek a broader audience for them.

Table Of Contents

Preface ix
False Prophets: They Tell Us What We Want
                           to Hear 15
False Prophets: They Give Us Something Tangible
                           to Worship 25
False Prophets: They Give Us a Man to Follow 37
False Prophets: They are Masters of Disguise 47
False Leaders: They are Ungodly Leaders 57
False Prophets: They Can Be Identified 67
False Prophets: Why They Fail 77
False Prophets: They Support One Another's
                           Iniquity , I 87
False Prophets: They Support One Another's
                           Iniquity, II 97
False Prophets: They are a Danger to the
                           Sheep 107
False Prophets: They Penetrate the Church in
                           Disguise 117
Essential Orthodoxy 127
At Ease in Zion 137
Christ Centered Preaching 147
Spiritual Effectiveness: Communication by the
     Spirit 159
Where Do We Go From Here? 169

Trojan Horses in the Church: A Preface

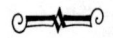

According to the legend of the Trojan Horse, the Greeks sought to conquer the city of Troy, on the west coast of Asia Minor, around 1200 B.C. When early attempts failed, the Greeks devised a crafty scheme to enter the city by deception. They built a massive wooden horse, which they offered as a gift to the victorious Trojans. Armed soldiers hid inside, intent on destruction.

Virgil described the scene in *Aeneid*, Book 2 as translated by John Drydan.

"By destiny compell'd, and in despair,
The Greeks grew weary of the tedious war,
And by Minerva's aid a fabric rear'd,
Which like a steed of monstrous height appear'd …:"

Notice the warning they received.

> "[...] Laocoon, follow'd by a num'rous crowd,
> Ran from the fort, and cried, from far, aloud:
> *'O wretched countrymen! What fury reigns?*
> *What more than madness has possess'd your brains?...*
> *Trust not their presents, nor admit the horse."*
> (Virgil's *Aeneid*, Book 2)
> (trans. John Dryden).

The trusting Trojans brought the horse into their city, not realizing that enemy troops lurked inside its hollow center. Under the cover of darkness, the Greek soldiers left their hiding place and captured the city of Troy.

In similar fashion, deceivers invade the Church of Jesus Christ today. Hidden in a disguise of positive energy and religious styling, they contribute to the spiritual decline of the Church through skillful misleading and betrayal.

Jesus warned believers of this danger in the Sermon on the Mount:

> *"Beware of false prophets, which come to you in sheep's clothing, but inwardly they are ravening wolves. Ye shall know them by their fruits. Do men gather grapes of thorns, or figs of thistles? Even so every good tree bringeth forth good fruit; but a corrupt tree bringeth forth evil fruit. A good tree cannot bring forth evil fruit, neither can a corrupt tree bring forth good fruit. Every tree that bringeth not*

forth good fruit is hewn down, and cast into the fire. Wherefore by their fruits ye shall know them." Matthew 7:15-20

This passage provides a very clear warning: "Beware of false prophets." They have existed covertly in every generation. In fact, we find in the Scriptures that this is a common warning.

The Old Testament describes at least four stalwart men of God who warned of the dangers of deceptive religious leaders. In Deuteronomy 13, Moses talked about the false prophets to come. Elijah made a spectacular appearance on Mount Carmel when he single-handedly slew hundreds of the evil prophets of Baal. We cannot forget Jeremiah, who frequently warned about them and gave some clues that described them and Ezekiel cautioned about them, as well. Throughout the Old Testament the Bible issues warnings about false prophets and teachers.

Jesus frequently spoke out against the Scribes and Pharisees, who were His contemporaries. Paul, the distinguished apostle, followed His example and warned against them. In his letter to the Galatians, he identified some of their characteristics. He wrote to his friend, Timothy, and spoke against the deceiving teachers present in the church under Timothy's care. The book of the Revelation of Jesus Christ contains strong warnings about untrustworthy teachers and leaders and how to identify them. Of the seven letters to the churches, six contain corrections about the false doctrine, errors, and treacherous teachers present in those churches.

The warning from the Lord Jesus provides a pertinent message for us. His admonition was necessary in that day, and is critically needed today. False prophets abound in the Church. They hold prominent positions of leadership as pastors and teachers. They profess to follow Christ but preach unbiblical messages that captivate the minds of the unwary and lead them astray. They write books and promote their counterfeit teachings using television, radio, and the internet. Their influence thwarts conformity to God's word. The Church today faces great injury because of their presence and influence.

Counterfeit leadership has weakened the Church, resulting in the disrespect of the world around us. The Church commands no fear and should be ashamed because of its inability to respond to public mockery of the Lord Jesus, the very Savior of the sinners.

The spiritual decline of the Church under the influence of misleading teachers grieves and quenches the Holy Spirit, and contributes to the ineffectiveness of the Church. We have replaced God's glorious, manifest presence with hype and emotionalism, pathetic substitutes for the real presence of God. Multitudes of the people who make up the congregations of our massive churches believe they have experienced salvation, but have instead followed heresy. They sit in comfort and confidence in beautiful church buildings, and they are lost.

Because of the prevalence of false prophets and teachers and their detrimental influence upon the Church, Christ-followers and His Church must heed the warnings of Christ. They must identify fallacious leaders, and refuse to follow them.

These studies warn of a contemporary Trojan horse. "Trust not their presents nor admit the horse!" The lessons presented in these studies provide Biblical evidence of the causes and conditions that give rise to false prophets. We will study the canons of Scripture as we examine the characteristics of misleading preachers and teachers. These studies will provide a Biblical course of action that will protect you and the Church from these current and damaging fallacies.

May the Holy Spirit use these studies to correct the Church and to call it to the revival it so desperately needs.

Chapter One

False Prophets: They Tell Us What We Want to Hear

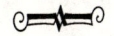

"I charge thee therefore before God, and the Lord Jesus Christ, who shall judge the quick and the dead at his appearing and his kingdom; Preach the word; be instant in season, out of season; reprove, rebuke, exhort with all longsuffering and doctrine. For the time will come when they will not endure sound doctrine; but after their own lusts shall they heap to themselves teachers, having itching ears; And they shall turn away their ears from the truth, and shall be turned unto fables." 2 Timothy 4:1-4

This section from 2 Timothy 4 describes the conditions and causes among Churches that give an open door to false teachers who have a form of godliness but deny the power thereof. These conditions permit them to foster their fallacies and errors, and enable them to step into the vacuum where they can assume positions of leadership and lead people astray. Those same conditions exist today, infecting the professing Church of Jesus Christ.

This passage of Scripture continues what actually begins in chapter 3 where Paul reminded Timothy of those in the Church who would love themselves, would not follow the truth, and would try to draw others away from the truth, *"Having a form of godliness, but denying the power thereof."* 2 Timothy 3:5 Paul responded to his young protégé, Timothy, concerning some of the difficulties that he faced. He wrote to instruct him on how to handle the conditions in the church where Timothy was pastor. He counseled him on how to live a godly life in his church and how to lead his people. The counsel that Paul gave to Timothy warns today's Church.

Professing Believers May Disavow Sound Doctrine

"They will not endure sound doctrine." 2 Timothy 4:3 Paul states—and he says to them very clearly—"There is going to come a time when people among you will disavow sound doctrine. They will go after that which is false, and they will not adhere to that which is true."

What does it mean when it says they will not endure sound doctrine? It means, very literally, they won't stand for it. They will not put up with it. They want something else.

What sound doctrine will they not endure? This means that they will not endure sound teaching. A little earlier in his first letter to Timothy, chapter 1, verse 10, Paul used the exact phrase "sound doctrine" and explained what it meant in verse 11. He stated that sound doctrine was *"According to the glorious gospel of the blessed God, which was committed to my trust."* 1 Timothy 1:11

The sound doctrine that Paul predicted professing believers would not endure, was the gospel. They would not endure the good news of the gospel that would save them and bring them back into relationship with God the Father. This group included not just those on the outside of the Church, but also those within the Church. He said that Church members and professing believers, who said they followed Christ, would not put up with the gospel.

We face a grave problem today, the misstatement of the gospel. The truths of the gospel are not proclaimed. They are disguised. *Part* of the truth is presented as the *whole* of the gospel. Therefore, many people falsely believe they have obtained salvation. They have accepted a portion of the gospel, not the whole gospel. They have never heard the gospel in its entirety.

For example, the modern day presentation of the gospel avoids the issue of sin, because people do not want to hear about their sins. However, the preaching of the gospel without including the truth of the sinfulness of mankind eliminates the key element of the gospel. The gospel provides salvation from sin. Sadly, many professing believers have never come to recognize their dire sinfulness before God, which is elemental to salvation.

Another often rejected portion of the gospel involves the truth that man contributes nothing to his salvation. One preacher said wisely, "The only thing that you bring to the salvation experience is your sin." Sinners, utterly helpless and dead in their trespasses and sins, obtain salvation only by a gift of grace from God. The presentation of the gospel today frequently excludes this truth. Most people assume that sinners supply something to their salvation. However, salvation is neither a cooperative nor a synergistic experience, one where each party participates on a sharing basis. Sinners contribute nothing to their salvation but their sin.

Leaders within the professing Church today follow the same practice that Paul warned Timothy people would practice in that day. They will not endure the gospel. They will not put up with it. They do not explain it in its fullness and all of its parts. This describes the first issue that Paul's warning to Timothy emphasizes, which gives rise to false prophets: people do not want the gospel.

Professing Believers Seek Personal Gratification

Modern day professing believers delight in satisfying their fleshly natures and desires: *"...but after their own lusts shall they heap to themselves teachers, having itching ears."* 2 Timothy 4:3 The phrase "but after" means they do not want this, but they do want something else. They did not want a spiritual emphasis in their lives, but they greatly enjoyed pursuing pleasure, which captivated their interests.

Someone once described the Church as a mile wide and an inch deep. I believe today's professing Church today is neither a mile wide nor an inch deep. Professing believers, who lack interest in the spiritual condition of their lives, fill the Church. Holiness seems reserved only for the devout. Interest in knowing God intimately appears outdated. Unfortunately, many professing believers want to know God, as that song says, "at a distance."

They prefer a faith that does not interfere with their lives. They do not want their Creator to interfere with their lives. They do not desire the discipline of learning to walk with God in obedience and trust Him with their plans.

The professing Church lacks interest in a deep walk with God: understanding Him, knowing Him, and pursuing after Him. These people lack the desire to grasp the truths revealed in God's Word about God the Father, the Son, and the Holy Spirit.

To soothe their "itching ears" they "heap to themselves" pastors who tell them what they want to hear, who give them lessons on struggling with stress, managing their budgets, and raising their children. Instead of the gospel and holy living, they want things that appeal to their natures. These professing believers seek out teachers who would scratch their ears and make them feel good. These conditions give rise to false prophets and teachers.

The Bible expressly speaks against these demands. Paul wrote to his friends at Rome, *"I know that in me (that is, in my flesh,) dwelleth no good thing."* Romans 7:18 He warned them in chapter 13 not to make provision for the flesh: *"But put ye on the Lord Jesus Christ, and make not provision for the flesh, to fulfil the lusts thereof."* Romans 13:14 This reference refers to the rejection of the putting on of Christ, and the pursuit after satisfying lusts. Paul said, "Don't do that. That is not the way you should live as a follower of Christ."

The Bible describes many who delighted in pursuing after God. David in a number of writings in the Psalms expressed his passion: "I delight to do thy will O God. I delight in your precepts. I delight in your law." Psalm One describes the blessed man, the one who experiences the blessings of God, as one who delights himself in God's law. *"But his delight is in the law of the LORD; and in his law doth he meditate day and night."* Psalm 1:2 These represent a host of examples exactly opposite to what many in the professing Church follow today.

Note the consequences that Paul identified: *"And they shall turn away their ears from the truth."* 2 Timothy 4:4 One of the great challenges facing the professing Church today centers on the debate regarding the existence of truth. The world has tried to debunk and degrade the gospel of Jesus Christ for generations, saying that we cannot know truth. The world has said this for a long time. They have said, "There is no truth. My truth is just as good as your truth."

Of course, the world would say that. They do not want to believe God's truth, because it describes them as sinners in need of a Savior, and they do not want that. However, it becomes an entirely different problem when men and women, who profess to be followers of Christ, assume positions as leaders and pastors of churches and say, "You can't know the truth." Many leaders, respected by the professing Church, assert that "You can't know the truth." They write books, make speaking tours, pastor churches, and grossly mislead their followers.

In essence, they teach that every one can know *their* truth but cannot know *God's* truth. When a false prophet, teacher, pastor, or leader makes these kinds of claims, (s)he establishes himself or herself above God. They create a truth that they impose which is greater than God's truth.

The false prophet or teacher who says, "You can't know the truth" contradicts Scripture, much like the serpent in the Garden of Eden who said to Adam and Eve, "You'll not die. God has not told you the truth. I am telling you the truth. Believe me. Don't believe God."

On the night of the Last Supper, Jesus gave a series of messages to His disciples on a variety of issues. One of the greatest issues concerned the Holy Spirit in John 14, 15 and 16. Jesus called the Holy Spirit the Spirit of Truth. On more than one occasion, He called Him the Spirit of Truth and told how the Holy Spirit would guide believers into the truth. Christ told them that *"... when He comes, He will guide you into the truth. Many things I cannot tell you now, because you cannot understand them, you will not endure them, nor will you understand them.*

You cannot grasp them now. But when He comes, He will guide you into the truth." John 16:13

Further, Jesus said, "I am the truth." In His prayer in John chapter 17, Jesus talked to His Father and said to Him, "One thing you will do Father; *you will sanctify these people in the truth.*" John 17:17 The Bible presents each member of the Triune God, the Father, Jesus Christ, and the Holy Spirit, as providers, teachers, and revealers of truth. To declare that no one can know spiritual truth defames the triune God.

Untrustworthy teachers welcome the opportunity to encourage their followers to enjoy an easy and false doctrine. They do it subtly, carefully, and persuasively, so that it sounds like the truth when, in fact, it is error.

Professing Believers May Turn to Error

In the process of turning to error, many churchgoers will reject any interest in spiritual emphasis in their lives and will gather to themselves deceptive prophets who will deny the truth. Ultimately, they will turn to fables, imaginations, and stories. They will follow error, not the Bible. The Church has just begun to enter this phase of decline.

This is a warning to the Church. Professing believers must open their eyes to the truth. Believers can know the truth, and it will set them free. The whole sequence presented in 2 Timothy 2.3-4 describes some of the most recently published Christian magazines, and television and radio broadcasts. Many counterfeit spiritual leaders produce books and internet articles, and preach in churches and to vast crowds all over the world. Organizations have risen in the last few years for the sole purpose of presenting error as true Christianity. Deceiving teaching looms dark over the contemporary church.

Have you been deceived? Have you been lulled into considering that you cannot know the truth, that God does not demand of you total obedience and surrender of your rights? Do you pursue God and His righteousness above everything else? Can you recognize untruth when you hear it from the pulpit?

I urge you to bring these issues to the throne of God. Seek Him and His wisdom and stand for the inerrant truth of the Word of God.

Thank You, heavenly Father, for Your great grace in making provision for Your children by giving them warnings. In giving the warnings You present that which is true and that which is false and the consequences of that which is false. And, Father, by Your Holy Spirit, apply these truths in our lives, that we might be taught by them, encouraged by them, strengthened by them, reaffirmed in the truth by them, corrected by them, conformed more assuredly and more completely to the truth. We will give to You, Father, Son, and Holy Spirit all of the glory for what You accomplish. Amen.

Chapter Two

False Prophets: They Give Us Something Tangible to Worship

"And when the people saw that Moses delayed to come down out of the mount, the people gathered themselves together unto Aaron, and said unto him, Up, make us gods, which shall go before us; for as for this Moses, the man that brought us up out of the land of Egypt, we wot not what is become of him. And Aaron said unto them, Break off the golden earrings, which are in the ears of your wives, of your sons, and of your daughters, and bring them unto me. And all the people brake off the golden earrings which were in their ears, and brought them unto Aaron. And he received them at their hand, and fashioned it with a graving tool, after he had made it a molten calf: and they said, These be thy

gods, O Israel, which brought thee up out of the land of Egypt. And when Aaron saw it, he built an altar before it; and Aaron made proclamation, and said, To morrow is a feast to the LORD. And they rose up early on the morrow, and offered burnt offerings, and brought peace offerings; and the people sat down to eat and to drink, and rose up to play." Exodus 32:1-6

God brought the Children of Israel out of the land of Egypt where they had lived for about 400 years. With a mighty hand, He set them on their journey toward the land, which He had promised to Abraham, Isaac, and Jacob long years ago. To prepare the people for their journey, God met with Moses on the mountain and began to give Moses the law as recorded in Exodus 20.

Exodus 24 describes a glorious event in the life of this new nation. Moses, Aaron, Aaron's sons Nadab and Abihu, and 70 elders of Israel went to worship God. In an unusual expression of His love for His people, God allowed them to see Him and celebrate with the God of the Ages.

"...Moses, and Aaron, Nadab, and Abihu, and seventy of the elders of Israel...saw the God of Israel: and there was under his feet as it were a paved work of a sapphire stone, and as it were the body of heaven in his clearness. And upon the nobles of the children of Israel

he laid not his hand: also they saw God, and did eat and drink." Exodus 24:9-11

Out of that group, God called Moses to come up to His presence. Before Moses and his helper Joshua went to God, Moses left instructions with those he left behind: *"... he said unto the elders, Tarry ye here..."* Exodus 24:14 He instructed them to go to Aaron and Hur for counsel if any problems arose while he and Joshua were on the mountain.

These events led to the disastrous scene described in Exodus 32. The same privileged people who entered into the presence of God, saw Him, and celebrated with Him, demanded new gods. They saw God standing on a sapphire stone. They saw His wonder, majesty, and beauty. Shockingly, soon after these events, the Children of Israel cried out for new gods and new leadership.

This setting in Exodus 32 provides another clear picture of the conditions that give rise to false prophets and false teachers. Further examination will reveal that what happened then is repeating in the Church today. The behaviors recorded in Exodus 32 take place today in the professing Church on a vast scale. These events serve as a warning to alert us, and make us wise in our judgments regarding the conditions that foster the rise of deceiving teachers.

They Disliked Delay

"And when the people saw that Moses delayed to come down out of the mount, the people

assembled about Aaron and said to him, "Come, make us a god who will go before us; ..." Exodus 32:1

When my wife and I were young parents we provided our daughters a series of Bible story booklets and records called *The Purple Puzzle Tree.* [Concordia Publishing House (1971)] One of the stories entitled "God Is Not A Jack-In-The-Box" captured their attention. The writers vividly instructed children that God is not a toy who jumps when a button is pushed. They described a popular child's toy - a box with a clown or a little figure inside of it and a handle on the side. A few twists of the handle and out pops the Jack-in-the-Box.

Like children with their Jack-In-The-Box toys, the Children of Israel wanted God to respond to them immediately. When Moses delayed, they rebelled against him. They did not want to wait for him and God's directions for them. The same attitude has become one of the great evils present in the professing Church today, an unwillingness to wait for God.

The desire for instant gratification dominates the Church's plans. The desire for numerical Church growth prompts leaders into plans and programs designed to hurry the process. Many believers abandon spiritual growth because it does not happen quickly. Sunday School administrators appoint unqualified teachers rather than wait for God to provide qualified ones. Modern day Christians want a God that responds to their demands on the spot.

The Scriptures relate some dire illustrations of the disasters that come upon those who fail to wait. For example, the prophet Samuel, after anointing Saul as King of Israel, sent him away to the people. As Samuel sent him, he told Saul, "Now, wait for me. Wait until the day of sacrifice, and I will come and sacrifice."

As the day of the sacrifice grew near, Samuel had not yet arrived, and King Saul became fearful and anxious. Impulsively, he went ahead with the sacrifice on his own. At that very moment, Samuel arrived to offer the sacrifice. Because of he refused to wait for Samuel, God judged King Saul for his impatience.

Abraham and Sarah provide another vivid example of the disaster that accompanies dissatisfaction with delay. God had promised them a son. They desperately wanted the son that God had promised them, and they could not wait. Their failure produced the birth of Ishmael, which resulted in continual pain and suffering instead of joy.

In contrast, the Scriptures teach the great value in waiting. For example, God promised, *"they that wait upon the LORD shall renew their strength; they shall mount up with wings as eagles; they shall run, and not be weary; and they shall walk, and not faint."* Isaiah 40:31 Isaiah records another example of God's instruction about waiting: *"Therefore will the LORD wait, that he may be gracious unto you, and therefore will he be exalted, that he may have mercy upon you: for the LORD is a God of judgment: blessed are all they that wait for him."* Isaiah 30:18

Like the Children of Israel who did not want to wait for Moses and God's directions for them, the Church today does not want to wait for God. We want instant gratification.

They Disobeyed God's Commands

God had told the Children of Israel very clearly, "Don't make unto you any graven image. Do not make it of any bird in the sky, anything on earth, or anything in the heavens. Do not make any representation of God. Do not make them. You are to worship Me and Me alone." He could not have been more emphatic.

Prior to this occasion, the Children of Israel as a whole swore their allegiance to God. "We will worship you and worship you only. We will only follow you. We will not follow anyone else. We will only worship you." Soon after, with impatience they said, *"Make us gods that they may go before us."* Exodus 32:1 They violated the first and second Commandments.

The professing Church today disobeys God's law frequently when it comes to worshipping God, with many excuses for these false practices. "If it only brings in one lost soul, isn't it worth it?" "Anything is worth one soul, isn't it?" These errors gain acceptance, because they appeal to feelings. The Church eagerly accepts almost any means that we believe will bring about numerical growth, even to the extent of violating God's law.

The Lord Jesus, in John 4, said to the woman at the well, "Those who worship me must worship me in spirit and in truth." What did He mean by that statement? God does not want believers to design trinkets, or images to facilitate our worship of God. This particular emphasis has experienced a sudden increase in the professing Church today. People flock to churches that make these things available as part of their worship. Such practices detract from the true nature and character of God and degrade Him into things made with hands.

They Deified Man

Notice what the Children of Israel said about Moses. *"He is the one who brought us out of Egypt."* Exodus 32:23

They attributed to Moses that which God had done. God brought them out of Egypt. He parted the Red Sea when Moses stood there quivering and wondering before God: "What am I am going to do?" God made the bitter waters at Mara sweet so that they could drink them. Moses threw the tree into the waters, but God made them drinkable. Moses did not provide the manna six days every morning of every week. God did. God caused the pillar of fire to guard them by night and the cloudy pillar to guide them during the day. God provided the water out of the rock to quench their thirst. The Scriptures record account after account of God's supernatural works on behalf of the Children of Israel, but they attributed them to Moses. They deified Moses and elevated him above God.

In a similar fashion today, the professing Church deifies its leaders. The Church desires leaders with glorious, wonderful personalities. They want pastors and teachers who will draw crowds and sway them with magnetic personalities and wonderful delivery. They have deified man and elevated him to the position above God. The Church does not want God anymore. It wants a popular man.

There are want ads in the back of Christian magazines advertising for pastors and Christian leaders that illustrate this trend. Rather than looking for Godly characteristics and experience with God, they concentrate on relevant work experience, education, ability to manage a multiple staff, and other human qualifications. In essence, they are looking for a man. Sadly, the Christian community has placed its emphasis upon man. Man directs the Church today, not Christ, the Head of the Church.

In the minds of the Children of Israel, Moses brought them out of Egypt. He made provisions for their needs. He performed miracles. That describes the pattern in the professing Church. The Church wants a Moses, somebody to lead it into the new millennium of the Church. Simply, the Church deifies man and rejects God.

They Disdained Godliness

The text says, *"As for this Moses, the man that brought us up out of the land of Egypt, we [know] not what is become of him."* Exodus 32:23

They saw God. They saw Him standing on the sapphire stone. Then, they saw Moses go up into the mountain to meet with God. They knew where

Moses had gone, but they preferred that he stay with them. They had disdain for Godliness.

The Pastoral Search Committees of congregations looking for a pastor do not seem to desire a man of God. They do not require a man of prayer, who will spend hours on his knees beseeching God to meet the needs of his congregation. They do not seek a man who walks with God, who knows Him intimately, and can share that with them and guide them into that same pursuit.

Several years ago, my wife served as a secretary of a large church. On one occasion, as the pastors of that church gathered to spend some time in prayer, she received a phone call from one of the members of the church. The caller asked to speak with one of the pastors.

My wife replied, "I'm sorry. He cannot come to the phone right now. He is in a prayer meeting with the other pastors."

The caller replied, "What do you mean he is in a prayer meeting? He ought to be working."

Sadly, that describes the attitude of many in the Church today. Few members realize the absolute necessity of their leaders spending time alone with God. Worse yet, few pastors and leaders recognize its importance. Too often, schedules, demands, and activities have a higher priority than time with God.

Years ago, I served on a pastoral search committee of my church. The committee established a list of criteria for the new pastor, which emphasized the very issues mentioned earlier in this study. At that time, I joined in the chorus of agreement with the list...until we met one of the candidates. I will never forget him. It was, I am sure, God's appointment to bring that man in as a candidate just for me, because that interview changed my life.

I will never forget that meeting. As the committee questioned the candidate on every conceivable issue, he gave the same response. After every question, he gave his answer to the question, then finished with this statement, "...but the most important thing is this. What are you doing with Jesus? Are you walking with Jesus? Have you yielded your life to Christ? Is He working in your life on a day-to-day basis? That is the most important issue."

God used that man's statements to change my life. Sadly, the church rejected him as the pastor because of his responses to the committee's questions. One of the respected leaders on the committee swayed the congregation with this statement, "Well, you know, we really do need a whole lot more than just hearing messages about Jesus."

That attitude permeates the professing Church today. It does not want a godly man. More than any other qualification, the Church needs leaders and pastors who know God. The Church needs to hear from those who have an intimate relationship with God, who spend time on their knees and on their faces before God beseeching Him on behalf of the church, trying to know Him, trying to understand Him. That describes the leaders and pastors we need today. Nevertheless, like the Children of Israel of old, the professing Church today disdains Godliness in its leaders.

They Denied Glory to God

After Aaron fashioned for them the idol from the gold that they brought to him, they worshiped it. They said, "These be the gods that brought us out of Egypt." After all of the wondrous displays of God that they observed, His nature, and His supernatural works on their behalf, they took a chunk of gold, worshipped it, and said, "That is what brought us out of Egypt." They denied God the glory that He alone deserved.

The professing Church of Jesus Christ does the same thing today. It gives honor to programs. It gives honor to books and systems. It praises the men. It does not give all glory to God.

The Bible warns believers that God will not share His glory with another. Thousands of years ago, the Israelites denied glory to God for His works and He judged them for their sin. The Church today follows in their footsteps. God is now withdrawing His glorious presence and has begun to judge the house of God. The Church must awake to its condition and seek God for remedy.

Thank You, heavenly Father, for this example that You have given us in Your Word of the failure of your chosen people to follow after You and in choosing the idols and choosing of leaders that would be other than the ones that You had in mind for them. I pray that You would teach us from it and conform our lives to the truth. In Jesus' name, Amen.

Chapter Three

False Prophets:
They Give Us a Man to Follow

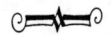

"And it came to pass, when Samuel was old that he made his sons judges over Israel. Now the name of his firstborn (of Samuel) was Joel; and the name of his second, Abiah: they were judges in Beersheba. And his sons walked not in his ways, but turned aside after lucre, and took bribes, and perverted judgment. Then all the elders of Israel gathered themselves together, and came to Samuel unto Ramah, And said unto him, Behold, thou art old, and thy sons walk not in thy ways: now make us a king to judge us like all the nations. But the thing displeased Samuel, when they said, Give us a king to judge us. And Samuel prayed unto the LORD. And the LORD said unto Samuel, Hearken unto the voice of the people in all that they say unto thee: for they have not rejected thee, but they

have rejected me, that I should not reign over them. According to all the works which they have done since the day that I brought them up out of Egypt even unto this day, wherewith they have forsaken me, and served other gods, so do they also unto thee. Now therefore hearken unto their voice: howbeit yet protest solemnly unto them, and shew them the manner of the king that shall reign over them." 1 Samuel 8:1-9

Without children, Hannah prayed earnestly for a son, and God gave her Samuel. At a very early, tender age, she took him to the Temple. He grew up in the Temple under Eli the High Priest and became a worthy prophet of God.

Eli, the High Priest, and his sons died in shame. In time, Samuel's sons shamed their father, too. When God uses a father in a ministry, people commonly assume that He will also use his sons. However, that is an incorrect assumption. Too often, a church follows an automatic progression from father to son. In this situation, neither the sons of Samuel nor the sons of Eli experienced God's blessings in ministry. These men with godly fathers did not seek God.

Give Us a King

With an absence of leadership, the people cried for a king. Circumstances provided a legitimate time to begin looking for another leader, but the comments of the people offer a glimpse into their real desires. Samuel warned them that their kings would burden them and bring them grief, and a long line of ungodly kings proved him right.

The Church follows a similar pattern today. As in the days of the fledgling nation of Israel, it desires a man to lead them. The choice of a man brings sorrow and spiritual decline. Man does not rule by grace, mercy, or justice. Wolves in sheep's clothing lead the sheep astray. They cleverly give the people what they desire. The people are pleased with such leaders and encourage them to assume positions of leadership in the Church.

When the Children of Israel came to Samuel, they did not ask for another prophet. They disregarded a godly man. Throughout their history, God had sent them godly leaders. When they were in Egypt, He sent them Moses, who led them out of Egypt though the wilderness to the brink of the Promised Land. Then, He replaced Moses with another godly man, Joshua. The time of the judges came after the death of Joshua.

During that era, God raised judges to rule and defend the Israelites. The book of Judges records numerous times that God lifted up judges, giving them unique abilities and strengths for their welfare and direction. He used them to bring the Children of Israel back to Him. Then came Samuel to lead God's people.

Samuel rehearsed to them what would happen, if they raised up for themselves a king. Verses 10-18 record his warnings. But, they turned aside from his warnings: *"Nevertheless the people refused to obey the voice of Samuel; and they said, Nay; but we will have a king over us."* 1 Samuel 8:19

They did not ask for a Godly man. Instead of praying for a Godly leader, they desired someone to go out and fight their battles. They wanted a leader who would wear a crown and dress in purple robes. They wanted a champion that would lead them as other pagan kings in their day.

These events describe the professing Church today. In place of a godly man, it wants a king to fight its battles. As the Church turned aside from seeking godly leaders, it substituted pizzazz and personality. A new list of characteristics demands a counselor, conciliator, a good businessman. These marks identify the kind of leaders that the Church wants. The Church no longer desires a man who communes with God. Like the Children of Israel, the Church today disregards godly men for its leaders.

Give the Majority What They Want

They made their decisions based on popularity. As you read the whole passage, mark the frequent references to "the people." En masse, the people came to Samuel and demanded a king. Popularity justified their actions in their cry for a king.

Presently, the professing Church has made the decision that popularity equals God's way. A vote with a high percentage confirms the Church's determination of God's will. Christ's kingdom is not a democracy. The kingdom of Christ has a King in charge. His name is Jesus. He rules as Head of the Church, His body. We need to determine what King

Jesus wants to do, not what the people want to do. He is the King. He is in charge of the Church.

A church that I attended a number of years ago had a practice that describes this custom. When it came time to select candidates for various church offices, they would seek candidates from each of the Sunday School classes and church organizations. They wanted to make sure that they had representatives from every group of people in the church. They wanted to be fair to every church group rather than selecting based on the godliness of the candidates.

That is not how Jesus rules. He is in charge, and He is the King. The Church is an organism, not an organization. We do not need a CEO, a champion, or someone powerfully persuasive in his personality. We need leaders filled with the Holy Spirit, leaders who spend their time calling upon God and seeking His face. When that kind of leader stands before the church and says, "This is the way. Walk ye in it," the congregation can trust their godly leaders. God's way is not decided by majority vote or by a committee gathered from of the various groups within a congregation.

Give Us Modern Methods

The Children of Israel cried, "We want a king." Where did they get that idea? They determined that they wanted to imitate the world around them. They wanted a king just like everybody else. They saw how the world managed their affairs, and preferred it to God's way.

At the risk of repetition, that describes the Church today. Its leaders try to exceed one another in their pursuit of discovering the world's latest methods and incorporating them into the activities of the Church. They want to follow the world's practices. They assume that if it works for big business, it must work for the Church. Like the Children of Israel, the Church of today wants to fit in and appease the world.

God does not work that way. The Scriptures tell us to come out from among them and be separate. Scripture never encourages us to go to the world to find out how we are to live as Christians. Further, Scripture never encourages believers to compromise with the world in order to win the world. The Church is supposed to stand against the world and expose its darkness. Believers should walk as children of light, not as children of darkness.

These three truths, demonstrated in Israel's cry for a king, suggest serious implications for the Church today. The Apostle John issued a serious comment regarding the relationship between God and the world. He said, *"Love not the world, neither the things that are in the world. If any man love the world, the love of the Father is not in him."* I John 2:15

Many leaders and pastors ignore this warning by pursuing the world's methods and manners while at the same time attempting to receive God's blessing over their plans. To love the world's methods and practices, and to continue to pursue them and their adoption, casts doubt upon the activities of these leaders. It calls into question the true nature and existence of their love for God.

Jesus warned that you cannot serve two masters. He will have no competitors in the operation of His Church. Scripture warns us of the true nature of the world: *"For all that is in the world, the lust of the flesh, and the lust of the eyes, and the pride of life. And the world passeth away, and the lust thereof: but he that doeth the will of God abideth for ever."* 1 John 2:16-17

James in his epistle described the distinction between earthly, sensual, devilish wisdom and God's wisdom. He began the passage with these words: *"Who is a wise man and endued with knowledge among you? Let him shew out of a good conversation his works with meekness of wisdom."* James 3:13 He then described worldly wisdom, after which he concluded: *"This wisdom descendeth not from above, but is earthly, sensual, devilish."* James 3:16

In contrast, James denoted a list of characteristics, qualities, and features of the wisdom that God sends. At the very top of the list, he identified purity, which literally means that purity is the number one characteristic of God's wisdom. Purity does not deceive. Purity does not a lie, nor conflict with Scripture. Purity is truthful, and honest.

There is a difference between the world's wisdom and God's wisdom. We need to recognize and pursue God's wisdom. The Church must heed God's wisdom. By so doing, we would reject the plans and purposes of the false prophets today, as well as those who propose them.

Scripture tells us that God will not share his glory with another. As you read Scripture, you will find repeatedly that God always does things in such a way that only one person will receive the honor and the glory, God. In Zechariah 4, we read God's message to Zerubbabel, who faced a difficult challenge. God assured him, *"This is the word of the LORD unto Zerubbabel, saying, Not by might, nor by power, but by my spirit, saith the LORD of hosts."* Zechariah 4:6 When something must be done, God will do it.

The example of the Children of Israel provides sobering insight into the circumstances that foster the rise of false prophets and leaders. We erroneously think the crowd must be right. We imagine that so many people cannot be wrong. Yet, might does not necessarily make right. The paths that seem right lead to destruction.

The Scriptures say that God perfects His strength in human weakness. His strength does not come alongside man's strength. We experience the fullness of God's strength, power, and ability in utter helplessness and weakness. I pray that the Holy Spirit will open your eyes to see the truth, draw you into the truth, and encourage and strengthen you with it. I pray that you will walk as children of light and not as children of darkness.

Father, thank You for this setting of the people crying to Samuel for a king because it so clearly illustrates to us the forces that we see at work within those who profess to be followers of Christ today. They serve to us as a clear warning: That is not Your way. That is not how You do things. Therefore, we can eliminate and reject those temptations, urgings, and prompt-

ings that we may have and pursue after You and permit You to reign over us as king.

Teach us, Father, by Your Spirit, how to follow the King, how to hear His voice through Your Spirit, how to tell the difference, how to discern the truth. There are so many voices today. Help us to hear Your voice and to follow it.

Father, we want to honor and glorify Your name in all that we do. We will give You praise, Father, Son and Holy Spirit, for what You accomplish in our lives to the glory of the Father and of his Son and of Your Holy Spirit. Amen.

Chapter Four

False Prophets:
They are Masters of Disguise

"Beware of false prophets, which come to you in sheep's clothing, but inwardly they are ravening wolves. Ye shall know them by their fruits. Do men gather grapes of thorns, or figs of thistles? Even so every good tree bringeth forth good fruit; but a corrupt tree bringeth forth evil fruit. A good tree cannot bring forth evil fruit, neither can a corrupt tree bring forth good fruit. Every tree that bringeth not forth good fruit is hewn down, and cast into the fire. Wherefore by their fruits ye shall know them." Matthew 7:13-20

This warning from the Lord Jesus regarding false prophets provides confirmation of their existence and a caution of their potential harm to believers. The Lord cancels all doubt regarding their presence.

They do exist, and He commands us to watch out for them and to guard against them.

Christ's warning provides four declarations to His followers for their protection. First, He emphasizes the duty of examination. Second, He identifies the deceit of the false prophets. Third, He enables the discernment or the discovery of the false prophets. Finally, He outlines the destiny of the false prophets.

The Duty of Examination

Since the Lord Jesus said, "Beware of false prophets," we dare not set aside that command. As followers of Christ, we have a responsibility to heed His caution.

Many avoid the examination of others, because they think that the Bible forbids it. They mistakenly apply Christ's teaching at the beginning of Matthew 7 to this issue, imagining that Scripture forbids judgment. However, a careful reading of Matthew 7.1-5 will show that Jesus did not forbid judging but instead gave direction on the *manner* of judging. In fact, the Bible frequently gives guidance in Romans, 1 Corinthians, I Timothy and Revelation on how to examine others and ourselves. We must approach it carefully, knowing that He will judge us in the same manner that we judge others.

Believers have a duty to examine those who come to them as teachers and assume positions of leadership in the Church. We must scrutinize their fruits to insure their authenticity, so that we do not follow false prophets. The devil and the pressure of

Wolves in Sheep's Clothing

the world have cleverly blinded our eyes and pulled us away from that responsibility. We must examine our leaders thoroughly, because Jesus warned us that false prophets would come. If we ignore this duty, we open the door to deceitful leadership.

The Deceit of False Prophets

Notice that in His warning, the Lord Jesus did not refer to a blatantly wicked, evil person. His warning was not about diabolically evil men and women who blaspheme against God. Instead, He talked about those who purport to *follow* Christ.

These false leaders say they are Christians. They claim to follow the truths of Scripture. They declare, "I teach you what the Bible says." We must examine our leaders carefully because counterfeit teachers come disguised as sheep. They look like sheep, but underneath they are wolves.

I do not know a lot about raising sheep, but I do know that no shepherd would want a wolf in his flock. As soon as a shepherd sees a wolf in his flock, he destroys him in order to protect his sheep. That describes the warning of Jesus. Wolves do not march into the congregation identifying themselves as wolves. They come disguised as sheep, professing to follow Christ.

Paul identified these kinds of false prophets in his day. He warned his friends in Corinth in a fashion similar to Christ's warning.

"For such are false apostles, deceitful workers, transforming themselves into the

apostles of Christ. And no marvel; for Satan himself is transformed into an angel of light."
2 Corinthians 11:13-14

When satan comes to tempt you, he does not always come in a frightening fashion, like the picture of the red devil with the pitchfork in his hand. Sometimes he disguises himself as good, even as an angel of light, a wolf masquerading as a sheep.

We need to evaluate teachers and pastors, televangelists and radio hosts. We have a duty to examine them lest we follow them to our spiritual harm.

The Discovery of False Prophets

Jesus taught us how to identify false prophets. Notice the picture that the Lord Jesus gave as the basis to show us how to make this identification. He taught us much with His example of fruit. He said, "You don't find grapes on a thorn bush" and "And you don't find figs on a thistle bush."

This is obvious isn't it? Fig trees produce figs, and thorn bushes produce thorns. Jesus went on to say, "Listen to me, good trees bring forth good fruit, not bad. Bad trees bring forth bad fruit, not good." *"You will know them by their fruits,"* He said.

To evaluate whether a prophet, pastor, or leader comes from God, we must examine their fruit. If the fruit of a leader is not good, we know he did not come from God, regardless of the extent of his skills and abilities. Good trees do not bring forth bad fruit. Bad trees bring forth bad fruit.

When He said that we would know deceptive leaders, He did not say we *might* know them, or we *could* know them. He said we *will* know them; more literally, it means we shall fully know, without a doubt.

A logical question, then, follows, "What qualifies as good fruit? How can we discern the good fruit from the bad?" A shortened list identifies three crucial criteria for spiritual leaders whether man or woman.

1. What does (s)he teach?

What does (s)he propose as doctrinal truth? True doctrine includes the sovereignty and transcendence of God, the deity of Christ and His atonement for sinners, and the inspiration and authority of the Scriptures. This doctrinal teaching demonstrates good fruit. If the person you are examining does not hold to these, you should suspect a false prophet. In later chapters, I will explain them more completely and include other crucial doctrines.

2. Examine the character and nature of the lives of the teacher or pastor you are following.

What is the persistent pattern and character of his/her life? A check of these matters will help you to evaluate the character of this person. The Scriptures teach us about the world, the flesh, and the devil, the three unholy temptations that come to us in life.

How does this person view the world? Does (s)he love the world? Does (s)he want to be like the world? Does (s)he encourage you to live like the world, to conform to the world to win the world? Television and radio personalities and many authors proclaim messages that emphasize these elements. They teach that as a Christian you can have all of the world's goods, and encourage you to pursue them, because you are entitled to them. They imply that it is your right and privilege as a child of God to have all of the abundance of the world, because God loves you and wants you to have it all.

Please take note of these warnings from 1 John:

"Love not the world, neither the things that are in the world. If any man love the world, the love of the Father is not in him. For all that is in the world, the lust of the flesh, and the lust of the eyes, and the pride of life, is not of the Father, but is of the world. For all that is in the world, the lust of the flesh, and the lust of the eyes, and the pride of life, is not of the Father, but is of the world." 1 John 2:16-16

The wrong attitude toward the world can provide a glaring signal of bad fruit.

Another character issue that signals bad fruit includes a person's attitude toward the flesh. What does (s)he say about the flesh? How does this leader purport himself or herself in the manner of life? Galatians chapter five enlightens us. Begin at verse 16 and you will read an explanation of the works of the flesh and a description of one who lives to satisfy the passions and lusts of life.

That section is followed by one that says, *"But the fruit of the Spirit is..."* The passage then lists nine qualities of someone who lives under the influence and control of the Holy Spirit. The difference between the two lists is like night and day. At the end of that whole passage, Galatians 5.24 says, *"They that are Christ's have crucified the flesh with the affections and lusts."*

Do you see the works of the flesh in the life of this person? If you do, that signals bad fruit. On the other hand, if you see the fruit of the Spirit exhibited in this person, that shows good fruit.

In addition to the world and the flesh, there is the devil. The Scriptures describe the devil in a variety of ways. One of them calls him the prince of darkness. Ephesians chapter six provides the hierarchy of the devil and all of the various powers that he has under his power and authority. One is called the powers of darkness. Do the characteristics that you observe in this leader suggest to you that this person has a dark side?

John in his first epistle tells us:

"This then is the message which we have heard of him [the Lord Jesus], and declare unto you, that God is light, and in him is no darkness at all. If we say that we have fellowship with him, and walk in darkness, we lie, and do not the truth: But if we walk in the light, as he is in the light, we have fellowship one with another, and the blood of Jesus

Christ his Son cleanseth us from all sin."
1 John 1:5-7

Jesus said in John's gospel chapter eight, *"I am the light of the world: he that followeth me shall not walk in darkness but shall have he light of life."* John 8:12 Is this person walking in the sunlight or in darkness?

3. What kind of fruit does this leader produce in others?

How would you describe the followers of this teacher? Do their lives differ in any way from the lives of unbelievers? Do they show an interest in leading holy lives? Do they demonstrate obedience to God? Do they show their love for Christ? Do they ever acknowledge the work of the Holy Spirit?

One last suggestion comes from Isaiah chapter eight.

"When they shall say unto you, Seek unto them that have familiar spirits, and unto wizards that peep, and that mutter: should not a people seek unto their God? for the living to the dead? To the law and to the testimony: if they speak not according to this word, it is because there is no light in them." Isaiah 8:19

Listen to what this leader says. Does it match up with Scripture? Does it fit what the Bible teaches?

If it does not, it is because there is no light in them. These are bad trees, bad fruit, bad prophets.

The Destiny of False Prophets
They are cut down and destroyed. Notice verses 21 to 23. Jesus described a day in the future at the judgment when many people will appear before Him, who will stand there and say, *"Lord, look at all the wonderful things we did in your name."* 2 Peter 2.1-3, 9. Jesus said He would say to them, *"Depart from me. I never knew you."*

They were wolves in sheeps' clothing, giving off the appearance of being a follower of Christ, even saying some of the right things. Jesus said that we would know them by their fruit.

As faithful followers of Christ, we must examine the pastors of our churches, the television and radio broadcasters, and authors of the books that we read. Do they reveal good fruit or bad fruit? Regrettably, upon examination we may find false prophets, whom we must no longer follow.

Dear Lord Jesus, thank You for this warning that You have left for us to beware of false prophets. We see many of them in our day. You told us they would come. You told us we would know them, that we could spot them, that we could examine them and discern the true from the false. Father, as we have examined this passage of the Lord Jesus teaching us, there is so much there that only the Spirit of God can open our eyes to see all of it, to understand any of it, and to apply it as we examine and follow the advice of the

Lord Jesus. I pray, Father, that You would pour out Your Spirit upon each one of us individually to teach us, to open our eyes to see the truth, and to discern light from darkness, good from evil, false from true, that we might know the truth, that we might follow after the Lord Jesus. We will praise you Father, Son, and Holy Spirit for what You accomplish in our lives, Amen.

Chapter Five

False Leaders:
They are Ungodly Leaders

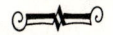

"And when the people saw that Moses delayed to come down out of the mount, the people gathered themselves together unto Aaron, and said unto him, Up, make us gods, which shall go before us; for as for this Moses, the man that brought us up out of the land of Egypt, we wot not what is become of him. And Aaron said unto them, Break off the golden earrings, which are in the ears of your wives, of your sons, and of your daughters, and bring them unto me. And all the people brake off the golden earrings which were in their ears, and brought them unto Aaron. And he received them at their hand, and fashioned it with a graving tool, after he had made it a molten calf: and they said, These be thy gods, O Israel, which brought thee up out of the land of Egypt. And when Aaron saw

it, he built an altar before it; and Aaron made proclamation, and said, To morrow is a feast to the LORD. And they rose up early on the morrow, and offered burnt offerings, and brought peace offerings; and the people sat down to eat and to drink, and rose up to play." Exodus 32:1-6

The Church faces a crisis in leadership. Evidence confirms that ungodly leadership exists in the Church today. Casual observation reveals a spiritual decline in the Church and in the lives of believers. Believers fail to walk in holiness and instead conform themselves to the world. Sermons preached in the pulpits of the American Churches today often explore psychology and the emotional ills of mankind. This emphasis attempts to use the Bible as a psychological textbook to answer these needs.

Theology and doctrine have come into disrepute. Pastors seldom present the challenges and corrections of sound doctrine. Instead, they emphasize a feel-good religion centered upon humanity and feelings rather than upon God and His righteous demands on us as His creation. Those who attempt to bring correction to the leadership of the Church today are sometimes condemned as out of step, creating dissension, and causing confusion in the Church.

The rise of untrustworthy leaders has played a significant role in the spiritual decline of the Church. We have grieved the Spirit of God and quenched His work among us. We lack God's glorious presence, supernatural authority, and ability that only His Spirit can bring to His people.

This Biblical account records a time when the Children of Israel faced a similar rise of ungodly leadership. God brought the Children of Israel out of Egypt with a strong hand. They saw His glorious presence on Mount Sinai. Then, Moses went up to meet with God, where he stayed for 40 days.

This setting provides a very clear picture of faulty, ungodly leadership and the problems that result from it. From this passage, I want to examine with you these characteristics described for us here. They provide insight into the conditions of the Church today and can protect us from their consequences.

While Moses talked with God on the mountain, the Children of Israel down below embraced idolatry. They turned aside from God Who had displayed Himself on the mount and revealed Himself to them in physical, tangible ways and with His law. They turned aside from Him to forge an idol. Aaron and Hur were at the crux of it all. When Moses went up on the mountain to meet with God, he left them in charge of the people. (Exodus 24)

Dread of Man

According to Jewish historians, when the Children of Israel grew restless and their faith wavered, they went first to Hur with a demand for idols. This man stood firm for God and refused to participate in the creation of idols. After this mention of Hur, he disappears from the pages of Scripture. What happened to him? Although the Scriptures are silent about Hur, most Bible scholars believe that the mob, frustrated with the strength of his resistance to their desire, murdered him. Next, they went to Aaron and gave him the same message, "Make us gods." Aaron gave in to their demands.

Several kinds of fear of man exist. One is very tangible, a physical kind of alarm, where we fear for our very lives. No doubt, Aaron felt this kind of fear.

There is another kind of fear prevalent in the Church today, however, an emotional, psychological fear. It is demonstrated in this way. Misleading teachers bargain in their hearts about what they truly believe and compromise on God's truth. They do not want to lose friends or families from the church. They want good attendance, so they yield in order to encourage their people to remain and visitors to come. They sacrifice the truths of Scripture and the promises they made in their youth to the God of their salvation in order to appear successful and appealing in the eyes of men.

They water down the truth. The dread of man pollutes their ministry. They fear that if they stand for the truth they will hurt people's feelings and some might leave the church. This emotional fear causes them to set aside the truth. They follow man, because they fear him, and they want to satisfy the crowd instead of God.

The Scriptures remind us, *"The fear of man bringeth a snare: but whoso putteth his trust in the LORD shall be safe."* Proverbs 29:25 Because of his dread of man, Aaron fell into a snare. Ultimately, he made an idol.

The Church must choose leaders who will tell the truth and minister God's truth with love. Sadly, many today display one of the clear signs of faulty, ungodly leadership: dread of man. They succumb to man's demands and desires instead of adhering to God's truth.

Disbelief in God

In this passage, we find Aaron following the world's methods. He devised a plan to get gold for the idol, he used his own skills and abilities to make the idol, and in the end, he tried to imitate reality by calling the idol, God. Throughout the entire episode of Aaron with the golden calf, he relied upon the world's methods and means. He simply followed the world's way of doing things, which he learned in Egypt. In his fear, he failed to trust God and instead, looked on the world's methods to solve the problem.

His carefully chosen words make it sound as if he is referring to God, but he gives the glory to a calf for bringing the Children of Israel out of Egypt. This gold figure, constructed of jewelry, was an appalling affront to almighty God.

In similar fashion, the Church today fails to trust God. We develop our own plans according to the world's patterns. Like Aaron, we leave God out of the picture. We adopt the world's procedures, ask God to bless our efforts, and imagine that God is glorified. We do not truly trust God and seek His will and purpose.

The Scriptures tell us frequently that when we rest upon the arm of the flesh we sin against God.

God reminded His children of this truth in Isaiah 31, *"Woe to them that go down to Egypt for help."* Isaiah 31:1 In Scripture, Egypt always pictures the world and the flesh. God says, "Don't go down to Egypt for help." Egypt has horses, manpower, and cleverness, but they cannot defend and protect you. God wants His followers to trust Him completely, not leaning on our own understanding or the current trends of our society. He says, "Trust Me."

At another time in the history of the Children of Israel, God told His people how He would help them. He said, *"And ye shall seek me, and find me, when ye shall search for me with all your heart."* Jeremiah 29:13

The Church today purports that they are trusting completely in God, but their actions do not indicate that it is a deep belief of their hearts. They start their services and meetings with prayer, because it is expected. They offer one or two minutes of prayer and feel they have given God His due, but their hearts and minds stray elsewhere.

That is lip service. That does not describe seeking after God with all of our hearts. To find God and His presence and plans, we must seek for Him with all of our hearts. God does not reveal Himself to the frivolous. He reveals himself to those who come to Him, seeking Him with all of their hearts.

Departure from Truth to Erroneous Doctrine

Because of his dread of man, Aaron made a false god. His disbelief led him to follow the rebellious people into idolatry. His departure from the truth caused him to take a dangerous step from God when he said, "This is God. We will worship him."

Toward the end of the text he declared, "Tomorrow is the feast unto the Lord. These gods brought you out of Egypt. We will worship this god." Aaron led the people astray with false teaching and false doctrine, and sacrificed the truth for the sake of peace.

Today, we often fall into incorrect doctrines in the same fashion as Aaron. We desire peace at any price, even if it means sacrificing the truth. Many leaders want unity so badly that they set aside certainty to get it. In our enthusiasm for the absence of controversy and contention, we set aside the truth.

That is neither unity nor peace. It is merely a cessation of strife. When you set aside the truth, you lose the basis for unity and true peace.

Scripture shows that Jesus did not make peace at any price. In fact, He often brought division among people by inserting the truth. Jesus said, "*I came not to send peace, but a sword.*" Matthew 10:34 The search for the truth brings temporary discomfort, but the truth will ultimately bring freedom. Unity and harmony will come as a consequence of the truth.

The Scriptures confirm this. The Lord Jesus warned his disciples about the leaven of the Pharisees, talking about their false doctrine. He said, "*Beware of the leaven of the Pharisees.*" Matthew 16:6 Such "leaven" causes dissension and problems.

The Word of God tells us how we are to respond to an intrusion of error into the Church. For example, in His letter to the Church at Ephesus in Revelation 2, Christ praised them because they put out those from among them who followed error and false doctrine. They stood for the truth and received commendation for it.

Later in that same chapter, the Lord Jesus pronounced judgment upon the Church of Thyatira. They permitted erroneous doctrine to exist within the Church. God does not want peace at the cost of truth. He wants the truth first.

If you have done any baking, you know the effect of a small amount of yeast. Just a very small amount of yeast in the bread dough affects the whole loaf. The Scriptures warn us that a little leaven, a little false doctrine, leavens the whole loaf. When we permit false doctrine to have even a small place in the congregation, it affects the whole body. That is one of the signs of ungodly leadership, following false doctrine.

The Scriptures tell us in the book of Jude that we are to contend earnestly for the truth. We are to stand up for that which is true from God's Word, and we are to resist the false doctrine. The call for truth often runs contrary to the Church today. Though those who call for truth may be called troublemakers, shunned by the congregation, they deserve respect.

Scripture tells us that we are to speak the truth in love, not anger, or contention. We are to stand for the truth in *love*, but we must demand that our leaders speak the truth, holding them accountable as God holds them accountable to the truth.

Under the direction of ungodly leadership, the Israelites, who had experienced the miraculous protection and glorious presence of God Himself, were reduced to pagan idolatry. Aaron not only permitted it, he participated in it. Let us not be satisfied with an Aaron. Let us look for a leader who will give us what we so desperately need and heal our Church from suffering.

Dear Heavenly Father, we confess that we have strayed from the truth. Forgive us our sin and guide us back to the truth. Open our eyes to understand it and enable us to conform our lives to it. In the name of Jesus, Amen.

Chapter Six

False Prophets: They Can Be Identified

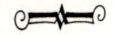

"The prophets prophesy falsely, and the priests bear rule by their means; and my people love to have it so...Jeremiah 5:31 Thus saith the LORD of hosts, They shall throughly glean the remnant of Israel as a vine: turn back thine hand as a grapegatherer into the baskets. To whom shall I speak, and give warning, that they may hear? behold, their ear is uncircumcised, and they cannot hearken: behold, the word of the LORD is unto them a reproach; they have no delight in it. Therefore, I am full of the fury of the LORD; I am weary with holding in: I will pour it out upon the children abroad, and upon the assembly of young men together: for even the husband with the wife shall be taken, the aged with him that is full of days. And their houses shall be turned unto others,

with their fields and wives together: for I will stretch out my hand upon the inhabitants of the land, saith the LORD. For from the least of them even unto the greatest of them every one is given to covetousness; and from the prophet even unto the priest every one dealeth falsely. They have healed also the hurt of the daughter of my people slightly, saying, Peace, peace; when there is no peace. Were they ashamed when they had committed abomination? nay, they were not at all ashamed, neither could they blush: therefore, they shall fall among them that fall: at the time that I visit them they shall be cast down, saith the LORD. Thus saith the LORD, Stand ye in the ways, and see, and ask for the old paths, where is the good way, and walk therein, and ye shall find rest for your souls. But they said, We will not walk therein. Also I set watchmen over you, saying, Hearken to the sound of the trumpet. But they said, We will not hearken." Jeremiah 6:9-17

During the time of Jeremiah the prophet, Israel progressed deeply into sin. Jeremiah chapter five recounts their injustice, hypocrisy, idolatry, and adultery. At the close of chapter five, Jeremiah identified the underlying cause of the people's condition in verse 31: "false prophets and priests." This passage from Jeremiah 5 and 6 records the character of the false prophets and priests of Jeremiah's day, who fostered and furthered the spiritual decline of Israel.

We can use the clearly described failures of Jeremiah's day to identify the false leaders among us and avoid the pitfalls that beset Israel. In this passage, Jeremiah identified six characteristics of false prophets and leaders. They aptly describe our era and its dangers.

Declaration of a False Message

When they said, "God said," they lied. They spoke their own messages. Further, when the priests failed to correct the prophets, the priests gained support from the prophets for their lavish, wicked lifestyle. And the people loved it that way.

This centuries old course of action repeats itself today. Counterfeit prophets abound with their messages of deceit. Their fallacies make void previously sacred doctrines such as the doctrines of salvation, the sinfulness of humanity, the authority of the Scriptures, and the nature of God. These represent only a short list of the doctrines they avoid to please people. Their disregard for truth has made their preaching a sham.

In similar fashion to Jeremiah's day, pastors and Church leaders today defend their erroneous beliefs for financial gain. They gain authority by the influence of human effort. Sadly, like Jeremiah's day, the Church seems to approve and applaud them. Scores of people find satisfaction and security in fallacies. Countless Church members cannot discern the difference between the true and the false.

Many who call themselves followers of Christ do not want to hear the truth. They would rather hear stories and problem solving techniques than messages on sin and the great doctrinal truths of Scripture. They have an aversion to sermons on the Lord Jesus and the holiness of God and His demands upon them. To satisfy their desires they look for teachers who will make them feel good. These erroneous endorsements further encourage the deceptive prophets to continue their sinful ways. (See 2 Timothy 4.3-4.)

Viewing God's Word with Derision

The shameful practices of Israel's leaders resulted in the people viewing God's word to them with derision. (See Jeremiah 6.10.) When God spoke to them through His prophets, the Israelites rebelled against Him and departed from His word fearlessly. Every level of society, rich and poor, defied God. His warnings fell on deaf ears and hard hearts. They had no interest in God's word. They traded God's word for that of the false prophets and priests. Naturally, this brought about a dearth of the knowledge of God. Doubt and unbelief followed.

In our day, we reflect the same attitude in a different fashion. We have replaced reliance upon God's word with books, retreats, and seminars to instruct and guide us in life. Persuasive leaders urge us to buy their publications and attend their meetings, with glowing promises that offer solutions to all of life's problems. Without exception, when people consult me with problems in their lives, they ask me to recommend a good book that will help them.

A friend of mine shared this experience with me. As a young man, new to the realities of life in Christ, he went to the one whom God had used to introduce him to these truths and asked him for a good book on them. After some deliberation, the man's teacher wisely replied, "I recommend a book that usually comes in a black leather cover entitled, 'The Holy Bible.'"

The mere writings of man cannot replace the Bible, God's word to humanity. He provided all that we need for life and godliness in its pages. Further, His words are alive. The writings of Godly men and women can help us, but nothing can replace God's word. God has not promised to authenticate man's writings, but He has given the Holy Spirit to illuminate our minds to understand His word and its role in our lives. As disciples of Christ, we must return to God's word and let the Holy Spirit instruct and edify us that we may grow.

Desire for Possessions

Verse 13 of this text identifies another characteristic of the false prophets, the desire for possessions. They loved money and sought positions of prominence. Their unbounded indulgences of the flesh drove them to dishonesty. Ultimately, their sin infected everyone, from the poorest to the richest, so that covetousness contaminated their whole society. No one denied their own selfish interests.

As in Jeremiah's day, this characteristic helps identify fallacious teachers. No doubt, you observe distinctive and well-known preachers on television and hear them on the radio. Have you noticed how many of them urge you to prove your devotion to God by sending money to them? It is interesting that they insist on money; no other demonstration of devotion will suffice, e.g., service or volunteer work. Further, these teachers entreat people to give money to *them*, not the local church or some other Christ honoring ministry. Such practices have become common in the Church today.

Dereliction of duty

False prophets in Jeremiah's day were distinguished by dereliction of duty. Verse 14 of Jeremiah 6 talks about healing the hurt of God's people slightly. Imagine a physician treating someone with a broken bone piercing through his flesh. Rather than taking the time and effort to set the bone straight, this doctor merely wraps it and puts a band-aid on the injury. This is an appalling thought, isn't it? Instead of really fixing the hurt, he just patches it up and hopes it heals a little. A legitimate spiritual leader, or prophet of God, demonstrates to God's people how hearts must be cleansed, sin eradicated, errors set straight in order for the Church to be healthy and strong.

In addition, God accused the false prophets and priests of saying, "Peace, peace," when no peace existed. The priests and prophets attempted to cover up their failures by proclaiming that everything was good enough. God said that no peace existed despite the declarations of Israel's leaders. Their problems were only slightly repaired.

Scripture records in other instances where God warned the leaders of Israel of their similar failures to address the true problems of His people. In Jeremiah 23, God likened the false prophets and priests to shepherds who scatter and destroy their sheep. In Ezekiel 34, God described them as shepherds who fed and cared for themselves, but left the diseased and broken sheep without care.

Today, many pastors and teachers follow the same pattern. They proclaim the same message: "Peace, peace. Everything is successful. There are no problems here." By avoiding the emphasis upon sound doctrine, God's people have become spiritually sick and malformed. Rarely do you hear a preacher over television or radio point out sin and call for repentance and reformation of life in conformity to God's demands. They heal the wounds of God's people only slightly, providing false help and hope. As in Jeremiah's day, this deceit fails to minister to the real hurts of God's people.

Defiance

When God chastised false leaders who had forsaken God's ways for their sinful acts, they responded with defiance. They experienced no shame for their sins. In fact, when their behavior failed to bring satisfactory results, they felt no disappointment or perplexity for their failures nor did any sense of humiliation lead them to repentance. They did not even blush.

This same attitude helps to identify corrupt leadership today. They indulge their appetites for money and possessions as if they deserve them. They even endeavor to defend their practices using Scripture. When their sin finds them out, they make mournful excuses for their behavior and strike repentant poses while continuing their life style. They reveal a disinterest in correction and repentance. Many defend themselves with the mantra, "The ends justify the means," as if stated spiritual aims can justify evil practices.

Denial of God's Ways

The errant prophets and priests of Jeremiah's day showed their true colors by a denial of God's ways. In verses 16 and 17, God instructed them through Jeremiah to return to the old ways and walk in them, but they rejected His demands. In addition, they refused to heed the warnings of the watchmen He sent to warn them. They refused to walk in God's way.

In our day, popular television and radio teachers evidently prefer the world's methods to God's ways. In their quest for crowds, they adopt worldly schemes that contradict God's word. They teach that our new day demands conformity to its mores in order to reach the current populace. They reject the old ways of God and replace them with tactics from business and politics. Calls for reform from Godly leaders who preach a return to Biblical teaching go unheeded.

Some say, "That is Old Testament. That doesn't have anything to do with us." To a certain extent that is true. We are studying Old Testament scripture where God was dealing specifically with the sins of Israel and of Judah at the time. He pointed out how the priests, prophets and kings failed to seek God, led the people astray and set up idols to worship.

Nevertheless, God has not changed. Although this prophecy pertains specifically to a time in the history of Israel, it gives us a glimpse into the heart and mind of God. He views the pastors and Church leaders of our day just as He did then. He will not long endure the foolishness that is going on presently in the Church. He is the same today as He was back then. He is not smiling and patting the heads of the pastors and teachers of our day who abuse the sheep.

There is coming a day when God will hold accountable the teachers, pastors, and spiritual leaders of our day for their sins. They have led people astray and refused to repent of their sinful behavior. They have not healed the hurts of God's people, and He will judge them. He will raise up shepherds who will feed the sheep and not themselves, who will fully heal the hurts of people. They will take care of believers and seek after the lost, too.

The Church today desperately needs revival. A few years ago, I talked with a pastor who spoke casually about revival. He said, "I have read a couple of books on revival, isn't it interesting?" Then he asked me "Why do you think we do not see revival?"

I forthrightly said, "It is because the pastors of our day do not have the courage to stand up for the truth." He turned his head a little bit and moved the discussion to another topic. It takes sacrifice to stand up for the truth.

There is coming a day when God will remove the counterfeit teachers and pastors. I pray for the day when He will install true shepherds in their places.

Dear Heavenly Father, we face a crisis in the Church today. Its believers follow in the footsteps of the false prophets of Jeremiah's day. I pray for mercy. I ask You to dethrone the false leaders and raise up those who seek after You and Your ways. I make these requests in the name of Your Son, Jesus.

Chapter Seven

False Prophets: Why They Fail

"Now the sons of Eli were sons of Belial; they knew not the LORD. And the priests' custom with the people was, that, when any man offered sacrifice, the priest's servant came, while the flesh was in seething, with a fleshhook of three teeth in his hand; And he struck it into the pan, or kettle, or caldron, or pot; all that the fleshhook brought up the priest took for himself. So they did in Shiloh unto all the Israelites that came thither. Also before they burnt the fat, the priest's servant came, and said to the man that sacrificed, Give flesh to roast for the priest; for he will not have sodden flesh of thee, but raw. And if any man said unto him, Let them not fail to burn the fat presently, and then take as much as thy soul desireth; then he would answer him, Nay; but thou shalt give it me now: and

if not, I will take it by force. Wherefore the sin of the young men was very great before the LORD: for men abhorred the offering of the LORD." 1 Samuel 2:12-17

It will interest you that this text was written during the life of Samson. God had instituted judges for Israel soon after the Children of Israel possessed the Promised Land that God had promised to Abraham, Isaac, and Jacob. You may know the story of Samson, the strong man who had great strength and performed wonderful feats of strength on behalf of the Children of Israel. Tragically, he sinned, and God permitted the Philistines to take him captive. They put out his eyes and made him a galley slave, grinding out their corn. Samson judged Israel at the end of Eli's tenure as High Priest.

Eli served as high priest over Israel. He had two sons, Hophni and Phinehas, who served with him as priests in the Temple. This record gives an account of these derelict sons. It helps us in the discovery of false prophets. The lives, ministry, and deportment of Hophni and Phinehas give indications of their true nature. This account of Eli and his two sons, plus a few other complimentary references, provide five different criteria by which we can discern failure in the spiritual leadership of the Church of Jesus Christ.

Dearth of the knowledge of God

Verse 12 describes a dearth of the knowledge of God. This word "knew" can be interpreted two ways. One way expresses factual knowledge, e.g., book knowledge, understanding, or some kind of insight into a subject. In this way, you can recite information about different matters with some degree of mental acuity, and a level of intelligence. With this knowledge acquired by observation and reflection you can say, "I know it."

That kind of knowledge does not define the kind of knowledge meant by "knew" in this verse. In this instance, the word depicts an intimate, personal relationship, an intimacy of knowledge by experience, a fellowship.

The two sons of Eli did not know God in that fashion. They had no intimate, experiential knowledge of Him. Because they had no personal relationship with God, they did not know Him. They may have known some facts about Him. Perhaps they could recount the story of God's appearing on the mount to speak to Moses, and give him the law. They may have been able to tell about the time God brought the Children of Israel out of Egypt, across the Red Sea, through the wilderness, and into the Promised Land. They could tell some things about God, but they did not experience a personal knowledge of Him. They did not truly worship or obey God.

This illustrates a warning concerning men and women who are recognized as having authority and leadership — those who are acclaimed as leaders in the Church. It may be that they do not know God. They may know about Him. They may describe facts about him. They may tell stories from the Bible. They have some level of knowledge about him. Sadly, some such leaders do not know Him.

The priorities and practices of counterfeit leaders reveal it. They take no time to spend in prayer and intimate fellowship with God. These spiritual leaders, on average, spend five minutes a day in prayer, seeking God's face. Further, the content of their preaching and teaching, as well as the absence of the unction of the Holy Spirit upon it, confirms their lack of knowledge of God. They do not know Him.

One cannot teach what one has not experienced. Neither can leaders guide others to a spiritual level they have not attained. People who follow many of our leaders demonstrate a dearth of the knowledge of God and the lack of an intimate fellowship relationship with the God Whom they say they serve.

Disobedience to God's Word

Eli's sons disobeyed God's word in the manner of their sacrifices. They completely violated the manner prescribed for them as given to Moses by God. God stipulated the acceptable offerings, the sequence of the offering, as well as the portion of the offering reserved for the priest after the completion of the sacrifice.

In violation of God's decree, Hophni and Phinehas demanded their portion prior to the sacrifice. In addition, after the completion of the sacrifice, they stole parts of the offering for themselves. They had utter disregard for the law of God as well as for the people offering sacrifices. They dishonored the sacrifices and failed in their responsibilities before God. Eli's sons saw these sacrifices as an opportunity to satisfy their shameless desires with gratification of luxury.

Wolves in Sheep's Clothing

A similar attitude of entitlement exists among many Church leaders today. They obviously believe they deserve special treatment because of their positions. They enjoy lives of luxury. They command sizeable salaries and spend Church funds on expensive vehicles and palatial homes. Their opulent dress draws attention to their pride. To justify their largess, they claim a special authority and anointing for them to indulge their impious desires.

Frequently, these purchases are made from funds offered by believers, those who trusted they were making an offering to the Lord. Like the sons of Eli, the false prophets, teachers, and preachers of our day take these offerings for themselves, beyond actual need. As a result, people have come to abhor offerings and view them with disdain, just as they did in the time of Hophni and Phinehas. (See verse 17.)

Debauchery and Immorality

These practices do not describe the worst actions of these despots. In verse number 22 it says,

> *"Now Eli was very old, and heard all that his sons did unto all Israel; and how they lay with the women that assembled at the door of the tabernacle of the congregation."* 1 Samuel 2:22

In that day, not unlike our day, the women helped in the temple, cleaning, sorting, and organizing, and helping the priest. Some came to pray and worship. We read about Anna the prophetess who was in the

Temple when Mary and Joseph brought Jesus to complete the law of circumcision and to present Him to the Lord according to the Law. She is one who came to the temple to serve, honor, and worship God.

Eli's sons used their positions to take advantage of these women and abuse them sexually. Shamefully, this practice did not end with them. I have read of some in leadership positions in the professing Church today who have illicit sexual relationships with women in their congregations. Members of their families are similarly sinful. Sexual trysts occur between staff members who travel together to meetings that promise to "glorify and honor God." When implicated, they lie about their immorality and justify it as a means for their victims to come closer to God. Just like Hophni and Phinehas before them, they are false prophets, teachers, and pastors.

Disdain for Discipline

After Eli heard some of these stories and the reports that came back to him of his sons' behavior, he said to them:

> *"Why do you do such things, for I hear of your evil dealings by all the people? Nay, my sons, it is not a good report that I hear. You make the Lord's people to transgress. If one man sin against another the judge shall judge him, but if a man sin against the Lord who shall intreat for him? Notwithstanding they hearkened not unto the voice of their father."*
> 1 Samuel 2:23-25

Wolves in Sheep's Clothing

When Eli questioned his sons, they responded with a disdain for discipline. They did not care for their father's warnings and rejected his attempts to correct them. In so doing, they disregarded God's Law and His rule over them. They held themselves above the people whom they served, living as they chose without regard for God's law and those whom God would use to correct them.

Many in our day have elevated themselves to positions beyond correction. They, too, follow an "I am different" attitude. They do not use the Church the way God designed it. They set themselves above Biblical Church structure rejecting correction and declining direction and guidance from Godly servants. They deceive others in financial matters and violate the tax laws of our land. When admonished for their practices, they fail to repent of their sins of disobedience to God and their violation of the trust of others. Like Hophni and Phinehas, they claim special anointing of God and disregard the correction of others.

Dearth of the word of God

Look at 1 Samuel 3:1. Beginning with verses 17-22 of chapter two, this section of God's word describes the child, Samuel. It says, *"And the child Samuel ministered unto the LORD before Eli. And the word of the LORD was precious in those days; there was no open vision."* 1 Samuel 3:1

When it says that the Word was precious in those days it literally means scarce. Scarcity of something helps to determine its value. For example, people all over the world view gold as a precious commodity. They do so because of its scarcity and high quality. This describes other kinds of things that we declare as precious and of value because of their scarcity.

Because of the sinful behavior of Eli and his sons, the Children of Israel experienced the deprivation of God's Word to them. They did not have any open vision. In that day as in ours, the vision for God's people came from the spiritual leaders to whom God has given a vision of His plans and purposes. No one stood up and said. "Thus saith the Lord. Go this way." This dire circumstance followed the failed leadership of Eli and his two sons Hophni and Phinehas.

A friend of mine, who now dances around the throne of glory, used to counsel me, "Tom, water never flows above its source. A spiritual leader can never take people above his level of spirituality. They will reflect their leader. If you maintain a low spiritual quality, so will the people that you lead. They will never rise above you. If you are not a man of God, your people will not be people of God."

The depreciation of God's word in Israel came as a direct result of the spiritual failures of Eli and his sons. The spiritual decline of the Church today results from the same failures of spiritual leadership today. In the third chapter of his epistle, James warns believers of the responsibilities of leadership. Those who lead in the Church have great liability for their actions. Leaders face greater condemnation for their failures, because the spiritual condition of those who follow them will reflect the leaders' condition.

The scarcity of preachers and preaching compounds the problem. Pastors and teachers today concentrate upon psychology, emotional disturbances, and "How To..." messages on money and health. This emphasis has replaced sermons on foundational Biblical doctrines and personal holiness. Preachers and teachers today have abandoned preaching the world of God for "talks," making no clear statement of God's truths. As a result, the Church careens as a rudderless ship, without direction or standards. No wonder the professing Church has declined in spiritual decay.

The examples of Eli and his sons provide a vivid picture of the spiritual condition of the Church today. Therefore, we must examine those who lead us to escape the same destiny of those who followed them. The identification of their traits gives us guidance on how to discern false prophets and teachers. May God, by His Holy Spirit, open our eyes to distinguish between truth and error and escape the wolves in sheep's clothing who threaten to destroy us.

Thank you, heavenly Father, that You have provided for us ways in which we can observe and heed Your warning to us through the Lord Jesus to beware of false prophets, ways in which we can examine them and come to some kind of evaluation and understanding of whether these men and women truly are men and women of God. Help us to reject the false and to pursue after the truth. I pray that You will open their eyes by Your Holy Spirit to see the truth, to understand it, and to grasp it. Grant us by the power of the Holy Spirit to conform our lives to the truth, to come to know You intimately, and to fellowship with You intimately. We will give You, Father, Son and Holy Spirit, honor, glory, and praise for what You accomplish with the truth in our lives. Amen.

Chapter Eight

False Prophets: They Support One Another's Iniquity, I

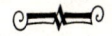

"And the word of the LORD came unto me, saying, Son of man, say unto her, Thou art the land that is not cleansed, nor rained upon in the day of indignation. There is a conspiracy of her prophets in the midst thereof, like a roaring lion ravening the prey; they have devoured souls; they have taken the treasure and precious things; they have made her many widows in the midst thereof. Her priests have violated my law, and have profaned mine holy things: they have put no difference between the holy and profane, neither have they shewed difference between the unclean and the clean, and have hid their eyes from my Sabbaths, and I am profaned among them. Her princes in the midst thereof

are like wolves ravening the prey, to shed blood, and to destroy souls, to get dishonest gain. And her prophets have daubed them with untempered morter, seeing vanity, and divining lies unto them, saying, Thus saith the Lord GOD, when the LORD hath not spoken. The people of the land have used oppression, and exercised robbery, and have vexed the poor and needy: yea, they have oppressed the stranger wrongfully. And I sought for a man among them, that should make up the hedge, and stand in the gap before me for the land, that I should not destroy it: but I found none. Therefore have I poured out mine indignation upon them; I have consumed them with the fire of my wrath: their own way have I recompensed upon their heads, saith the Lord GOD." Ezekiel 21:24-31

God sent Ezekiel to prophesy to the people of Israel who did not follow God. The nation, as a whole, had rejected and separated themselves from God. As a result, God sent Ezekiel to call them to repentance. This passage of Scripture records a summary of several messages that he gave to them as he described their sins and called them to turn from their wicked ways.

At the beginning of this message, the prophet reminded them of the reason for the lack of rain. God promised King Solomon that He would not withhold rain as a blessing for their obedience, but He *would* withhold rain as a judgment for their disobedience.

The prophet then described the sins of the prophets, priests, princes, and the general population that prompted God's judgment upon them.

Since Israel provides a vivid picture of the Church, we can learn by studying God's dealings with Israel. The present condition of the Church mirrors the condition of Israel described in our study passage. Like Israel, we experience a famine of spiritual rain. We experience God's judgment for our sinfulness. We have failed to follow God completely.

As Ezekiel explained to Israel their sinfulness, he specifically identified the presence of sinful leadership. As with Israel, the Church suffers from the disastrous impact of false teachers who have led the spiritual decline in the Church. Since God has not changed, we can use Ezekiel's message as a warning. He described the sins of counterfeit spiritual leaders, which contributed to Israel's deplorable condition.

Devoured Souls

Ezekiel said in verse 22:25 says, *"There is a conspiracy of the prophets in the midst thereof like a roaring lion ravening the prey."* Many of us have observed videos of lions pursuing their prey. Once the pray is captured, the pride of lions ravages the victim. That describes the action of the false prophets in Ezekiel's time. The history of Israel reveals several ways that the false prophets devoured souls. In the most obvious way, they destroyed true prophets. False prophets often killed a true prophet who contradicted them. Hebrews 11 recounts some of the ways they destroyed them. In cruel mutilations, they cut off their heads, drove swords through their bodies, or sawed them in half.

Defamed True Prophets of God
In addition, false prophets defamed the true prophets. They denounced their messages, mocked them, banished them, and punished them for their pronouncements. In some instances, they brought the prophets of God into the public square and put them in stocks. Passersby mocked them, because they had the audacity to try to proclaim the truth against the faulty leaders who controlled things. By their actions, these false leaders deprived the people of God's truth, leading to the devastation of the people and their lands at the hands of Israel's enemies.

Delivered incorrect Message of Peace
Further, the sham prophets devoured souls by declaring a false message of peace and prosperity in times of danger. Their troubled people needed to be warned, yet the misleading prophets said, "Don't worry. Everything is fine, because everyone is doing a good job. Things are good." But, it was a false message. In fact, the people faced extreme hardship, difficulty, and danger. The incorrect message of peace and prosperity ultimately led the people into destruction.

This happened in Jeremiah's day. He said,

"For from the least of them even unto the greatest of them every one is given to covetousness; and from the prophet even unto the

priest every one dealeth falsely. They have healed also the hurt of the daughter of my people slightly, saying, Peace, peace; when there is no peace." Jeremiah 6:13-14

Ezekiel proclaimed a similar message in chapter 13. He said, *"Because with lies ye have made the heart of the righteous sad, whom I have not made sad; and strengthened the hands of the wicked, that he should not return from his wicked way, by promising him life."* Ezekiel 13:22

Each of these examples describes events in our day. In many parts of the world, men and women lose their lives, because they proclaim the truth of God to their peoples. More Godly men and women have lost their lives for Christ in our day than in all previous eras combined.

Thousands suffer severe persecution. Even in our land, believers sometimes endure mockery and defamation because they stand for God. Some lose jobs and professional positions because of their love for God. Worse yet, some who stand for the truth in the professing Church face condemnation and exclusion from leadership.

Incorrect messages of peace and prosperity flood our and other countries as well. Religious television and radio broadcasts proclaim a false message of hope. Books and magazines publish these misleading messages. Our time of danger demands the truth, but fallacies and error overrun it. We need to return to the truth and to conform our lives to it.

The means by which prophets of Ezekiel's era devoured lives and contributed to the decline and the downfall of the Children of Israel exist in our time as well. We need to heed the warnings of Ezekiel to protect us from the same devastation that Israel experienced.

Divesture of Property of the People of God
The false prophets of that day made a practice of divesting the people of their goods and property. (verse 25) Ezekiel said they had *"taken the treasure and precious things."* Because of their lies and their presumptions of their positions as messengers of God, they stole from the people. They extorted money and property from them, especially widows, and by their deceits they pillaged the land and people.

The Lord Jesus specifically spoke about this very sin in Matthew 2. The Pharisees of His day devoured widows' houses. In the time of Jesus, they went to those least able to defend themselves and extorted from them their goods, lands, and their property.

Similarly today, many false leaders practice this same deceit. They ask members of their audiences a series of questions. For example, "Do you experience financial difficulty? Do you have debts that you cannot pay? Do your expenses exceed your income so that you do not have enough money to cover all of your expenses and your cost of living? Does that describe you?"

They say, "If that describes you, I have wonderful news for you. If you will send me a gift in the amount of your debt, God will bless you and will send you money 100 times what you send me." In this way, these modern day false teachers divest millions of people of their money and property.

These things happened in the time of Ezekiel and in the time of Jesus, and they are happening today as well. Do not follow such leaders. Yes, God did promise to provide for the needs of His children. However, when you hear or read someone who makes an offer that requires you send them money, turn them off and destroy their publications. God will make a way for you, as you trust Him.

Defense of Evil

The false prophets of Ezekiel's day defended evil for personal good. Notice what it says in verse 28.

"And her prophets have daubed them with untempered mortar." Ezekiel 22:28

If you go to verse 27, you will see what Ezekiel says about the princes, the leaders and the ruling people of their day. He describes the actions of the kings and their children and then tells how the prophets treated those princes. He says the prophets have daubed them with untempered mortar. What does that mean?

In that day when they made plaster for walls or structures, they used straw as a binding agent to help hold the material together and provide strength to the material. Maybe you remember the story of the Children of Israel as slaves in Egypt. They had to make bricks for the Egyptians and used straw in making them. When the emperor or Egypt wished to punish the Children of Israel he took away their straw.

That helps us understand Ezekiel's picture. When he said that the prophets daubed them with untempered mortar, he meant that the sham prophets propped up the princes, supported and defended them, but with untempered mortar that would neither last nor provide strength. It did not contain the substances that strengthens the mortar, so it wouldn't work.

The evil spiritual leaders propped up their leaders and the evil actions of the rulers with false supports for their own advancement. The rulers became like ravening wolves, shedding blood, destroying souls, and profiting from dishonest gain. (See verse 27.) The false prophets supported and defended them to the people. They proclaimed that God had given them directions to aid them in this manner, when He had not so ordered.

These offenses are as current as today's television, radio, and print publications. Ungodly men and women, who proclaim themselves as messengers of God, support one another in robbing the Church of godly leadership. Boards of Directors close their eyes to sin and corruption in the ministry and support figureheads who dangerously weaken the Church. Church boards defend pastors whose lives do not reflect the purity and grace of God.

The evil leaders of Ezekiel's day formed a conspiracy that resulted in the destruction of the land. Their actions give us insight into similar evil practices today. They serve as a warning to help us determine the true from the false. I pray that the Spirit of

God will open your eyes to discern the truth, so that you can reject error and pursue the truth.

Dear heavenly Father, I want to thank You for this record that You have provided and preserved for us from Your dealings with the Children of Israel in the time of Ezekiel. You have preserved it so that we can profit from what You revealed to him about the conditions of his day, because we see many of these same things present in our day as well. I would ask You, heavenly Father, to send forth Your Holy Spirit to teach us the truth and to open our eyes to see what Your Word describes for us that we might discern the false in our day, so that we may pursue after the truth. It will lead us to You, and to an understanding and knowledge of You through your Son, the Lord Jesus Christ. I pray these things, heavenly Father, in the name of Jesus, your Son. Amen.

Chapter Nine

False Prophets:
They Support One Another's Iniquity, II

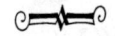

"And the word of the LORD came unto me, saying, Son of man, say unto her, Thou art the land that is not cleansed, nor rained upon in the day of indignation. There is a conspiracy of her prophets in the midst thereof, like a roaring lion ravening the prey; they have devoured souls; they have taken the treasure and precious things; they have made her many widows in the midst thereof. Her priests have violated my law, and have profaned mine holy things: they have put no difference between the holy and profane, neither have they shewed difference between the unclean and the clean, and have hid their eyes from my sabbaths, and I am profaned among them. Her princes in the midst thereof are like

wolves ravening the prey, to shed blood, and to destroy souls, to get dishonest gain. And her prophets have daubed them with untempered mortar, seeing vanity, and divining lies unto them, saying, Thus saith the Lord GOD, when the LORD hath not spoken. The people of the land have used oppression [or deceit], and exercised robbery, and have vexed the poor and needy: yea, they have oppressed the stranger wrongfully. And I sought for a man among them, that should make up the hedge, and stand in the gap before me for the land, that I should not destroy it: but I found none. Therefore have I poured out mine indignation upon them; I have consumed them with the fire of my wrath: their own way have I recompensed upon their heads, saith the Lord GOD." Ezekiel 22:23-31

In the previous chapter, we looked at this passage from the aspect of the prophets in the day of Ezekiel and examined the actions that made them false prophets. Ezekiel 22:23-31 reveals another part of the conspiracy, the priests. They also contributed to the decline of Israel from God, because they failed to fulfill their responsibilities before God to the Children of Israel and became corrupt, Ezekiel said,

"Her priests have violated my law, and have profaned mine holy things: they have put no difference between the holy and profane, neither have they shewed difference between

the unclean and the clean, and have hid their eyes from my sabbaths, and I am profaned among them." Ezekiel 22:26

They Disregarded God's Word

Ezekiel mentioned the priests' disregard of God's word in verse 26: *"Her priests have violated my law."* They treated God's word as if it were just another of the historical accounts of the Children of Israel that might provide interesting reading. They did not regard its demands upon life as important. Their misconduct resulted in both their defiance against God and the disobedience of Israel as well.

They nullified certain passages of Scripture involving the commandments of God. They set aside parts of God's word, because it did not fit into their current culture and desire. They disregarded God's law and His word.

Many modern day Christian leaders follow the same pattern. They, too, disregard God's word and misrepresent its application. They relegate whole portions of Scripture as relevant for years past, but not for today in our "new era." A theory of progressive revelation and conformity to culture writes off fundamental doctrines. They take a *part* of the complete doctrine and say "that's the whole doctrine." Denying part of the truth results in untruth.

God's explanation of the priests in Ezekiel's time describes errant leaders of today. They have set aside the authority of Scripture and violated God's word. Isaiah the prophet warned against this error when he instructed God's people to use the law and the testimony, the totality of scripture, as a standard to discern false prophets and reject them. (See Isaiah 8.19-20.) We need to heed Isaiah's counsel these days, too.

They desecrated the holy things. God described three areas in their actions where the false priests in Ezekiel's time profaned His holy things.

They Failed to Distinguish Between the Holy and the Profane.

This distinction separated the clean from the unclean. For example, God established restrictions on who could enter certain sections of the Temple. The priests of that day took no notice of those distinctions. Anybody, holy, clean, or unclean, could go anywhere in the Temple that they wanted.

In addition, God had established a series of animal sacrifices, clean and unclean, for the people to atone for their sins and to worship Him. God demanded the best animals. The false priests set aside God's rules so that the people could bring the sacrifices that they wanted to bring, sickly, lame, or malformed at birth. The priests of Ezekiel's day rejected God's requirements, which distinguished between the holy and the profane sacrifices.

In our day, misleading pastors fail to separate the holy from the profane. Although we do not have the same set of rules for Temple worship and sacrifices, some leaders today fail to distinguish between the holy and the profane. Specifically, they fail to identify and condemn sin. Preachers from the pulpits of our churches and from television programs, as well as popular authors, stay away from the whole issue of sin. The desire for popularity controls the issues. Some popular preachers present the gospel solely as a free pass to heaven and never even mention sinner's transgressions that needs forgiveness.

As in Ezekiel's day, we have failed to distinguish between the holy and profane, the clean and the unclean. As a result, the Church has declined into spiritual decay. We renamed sin and called it "a mistake or an error in judgment." However, God's demands of holiness of His people require that spiritual leaders preach on sin so that believers can repent. We desperately need preachers who proclaim God's holy demands.

They Failed to Worship God Truly

The priests of Ezekiel's day not only desecrated God's holy things when they failed to distinguish between the holy and the profane, but also when they failed to worship God truly. This sin developed because the priests rejected God's law regarding the Sabbaths. God instituted several Sabbaths, not just the one that occurred every seventh day. He set aside the seventh day as a day of rest and worship. God also established special Sabbaths with feasts and ceremonies, which called for the people of God to worship and celebrate God's goodness to them at various times and seasons. At these times, the people honored and glorified God.

As Ezekiel stated in verse 26, the false priests "hid their eyes from my Sabbaths." They set aside the ways that God had instituted for His people to honor, glorify, and worship Him. The result was a decline in true worship of God. The Children of Israel in the day of Ezekiel violated God's requirements.

In addition to hiding the Sabbaths, they completely rejected God's commands regarding idols. In disobedience to God, they built idols and elevated altars to them. They made groves throughout the land for their special gods. They ignored God's requirements for His people and designed methods and requirements of their own.

Jesus said that God is a spirit, and we must worship Him in spirit and truth. Yet counterfeit pastors and teachers of our day set aside this command. Much of what passes as worship today has become nothing more than hyped emotionalism, manufactured by stirring orchestral accompaniments led by enthusiastic choral leaders. It differs little from what occurs at rousing motivational seminars or exciting athletic events. Some have even recommended a return to the use of objects and ceremonies as part of worship of God.

The contemporary Church has set aside the importance of worship. We have trivialized the manner in which we acknowledge the holy, sovereign, creator God, Who holds our very breath in His hands and provides all things for us. Just as in Ezekiel's day, true worship of God has declined and virtually disappeared. We need a reformation of true worship of God, giving Him the honor, glory, and praise that He deserves.

They Dishonored God

The priests in Ezekiel's day set aside the distinctions between the holy and the profane, and the true worship of God, and in the end, they profaned God. By their dismissive attitude, they diminished the sovereign God. In fact, they had established other kinds of gods that they thought were equal with God. They set up many gods, such as gods of harvest, gods of seasons, gods of reproduction, as well as gods of the sun, moon, and stars. Eventually they just designated one title that covered a whole multitude of gods. They called them the Baals.

Worship of these false gods dishonored God. This same sin has begun to invade the professing Church today. We call it pluralism, which means that each person worships his own god in his own way. Any form of worship is acceptable. Some believe that people in other cultures or places may worship as they please, no matter whom they call "God." They suggest that it is unnecessary to reach the followers of pagan god's with the Gospel of Jesus Christ.

I have often heard the phrases, ""The God I worship is ......, " or "I like to think that God ..... " We have all defined an image God in our minds. Some prominent preachers and teachers even shamefully state that every religion has its own Jesus. They proclaim that God has other ways of salvation and will accept those of other religions based upon the sincerity of their beliefs, even if contrary to the truths of Scripture.

In all of these instances, the true and living God is no longer worshipped but profaned. He has revealed

Wolves in Sheep's Clothing

Himself to us in creation, our natures, and in His Son, Jesus Christ. He disclosed Himself to us in His Word, which we can read and study to learn of Him. He reveals Himself to us and requires us to worship Him and Him alone.

These characteristics of the priests in Ezekiel's day identify them as false priests, co-conspirators, if you will, with the false prophets that we examined in the previous chapter. The things that described them describe men and women in our day as well. These untrustworthy leaders of our churches, misleading preachers on television and radio, and authors of print media call on you to follow them. Examine them before you follow them, because there are consequences.

What affect did these sins have on the leaders of the people? The governmental leaders of that day followed the examples and the teachings of the false prophets and teachers, and became oppressive leaders. They developed into thieves, murderers, and deceivers who led the people into servitude, because of the sin and iniquity in their own lives.

The degradation affected the people as well. Verse 29 tells us that the people followed the leadership of the land and became like them. They, too, became oppressors, thieves, and murderers who destroyed the poor and the needy by failing to care for them.

Notice that what happened in that day happens in our day throughout the world. God has not changed. We will endure a similar judgment from God, if we, like the prophets and priests in Ezekiel's day, fail to honor Him and to seek his face. When we fail to worship Him in the manner He requires of us, when we disregard Him and set aside His word, God will withdraw His presence, and we will endure His judgment upon us.

I pray that the Spirit of God will take these truths and open your eyes to see them, to see how they apply to you. Perhaps He will show you where you need to turn from a path contrary to God's word. I pray that you will experience the forgiveness and the restoration that God has promised to those who repent.

Thank You, heavenly Father, for the examples that You give us in Your Word to warn us and encourage us to examine our lives and to see if we have failed to obey and failed to worship You as You require. I pray that we will see how we need to conform our lives to the truth, to obey, follow, and to worship You. I pray, Father, that You will accomplish this in our lives to the honor and glory of Your name. I pray these things in the name of Jesus, Your Son, Amen.

Chapter Ten

False Prophets: They are a Danger to the Sheep

"And as he sat upon the mount of Olives, the disciples came unto him privately...Matthew 24:3 Tell us, when shall these things be? and what shall be the sign of thy coming, and of the end of the world? And Jesus answered and said unto them, Take heed that no man deceive you. For many shall come in my name, saying, I am Christ; and shall deceive many... Matthew 24:3-5 And many false prophets shall rise, and shall deceive many...Matthew 24:11 Then if any man shall say unto you, Lo, here is Christ, or there; believe it not. For there shall arise false Christs, and false prophets, and shall shew great signs and wonders; insomuch that, if it were possible, they shall deceive the very elect. Behold, I have told you before[hand]."
Matthew 24:23-25

These scattered verses within Matthew 24 relate to the dangers of imposters to Christ's disciples. If you go back a couple of chapters to Matthew 21, you will read the parable that Jesus gave a group of men including His disciples, the chief priests, and the Pharisees. His story described the condition of the Children of Israel.

A householder owned some land and sent messengers to evaluate those whom the landowner had placed in care of the crops. Those left in charge of the crops killed all of the messengers sent by the landowner to assess the managers and the crops.

Finally, the landowner sent his son to check up on the property and those who tended it. When those left in charge of the property saw the son coming, they recognized him and said, "This is the son of the owner. Let's get rid of him, and then everything will be ours." So, they murdered the son of the landowner as well.

At the end of the parable, Jesus asked, "What do you think the landowner will do when he comes back himself and checks up on those to whom he entrusted his property?"

Immediately they shouted back, "He will destroy them, and he will take away what he had entrusted to them and give it to someone else."

I can imagine that Jesus sternly pointed his finger at these men and said, "That will happen to this generation. The kingdom that was given to you will be taken away from you and given to someone else."

Then it says that his listeners knew His threat applied to them. They knew the meaning of that parable.

At the end of chapter 23, Jesus concluded a strong sermon against the scribes and Pharisees and denounced them for their hypocrisy. He closed His message to them with the reminder that they had persecuted and killed the prophets and messengers He had sent to speak to them. Then Jesus told them, *"Because you have done that to My messengers, the very blood of everyone from Abel up through the Zacharias, all of the blood of all those prophets and messengers that I sent unto you, will come upon you, because you have rejected the messengers that I sent unto you. It shall happen to this generation."*

That provides the background to Matthew 24:3 in which Jesus foretold of the destruction of the Temple. After hearing these messages, Christ and His disciples spent some private time together, and they asked Him, "When will this happen?"

At this point Jesus said, "Take heed, listen..." He gave them a warning regarding false prophets. He told them of the presence and the increase of false prophets. Imposters have existed through the succeeding centuries, not only during the time that Jesus described in Matthew 24. In fact, we have false prophets and teachers in our day, and we can learn from Christ's warning. We must apply this truth to our day, so that we will be protected from deception.

Before we examine the warning about false prophets, we need to recognize two things. First, the phrase "Take heed" not only means "Beware, look out for" but also "Discern." His warning carried two meanings. As He presented His warning, Jesus provided several characteristics about false prophets that will help the Church today resist them.

The Sure Presence of False Prophets

Jesus did not say that false prophets *might* come. He said they *would* come. It was a certainty. Biblical and Church history confirmed this statement. God's people have always faced false leaders, centuries before Christ and after Him as well. They still exist today.

The Prevalence of False Prophets

Some might imagine that these imposters would appear occasionally - a few "kooks" and "nuts" with emotional instabilities. In that case, you might just dismiss them easily. However, Christ warned that many would come. The condition of today's Church not only verifies their presence but their prevalence. Many false teachers and leaders confuse believers and lead them astray.

The Persuasiveness of False Prophets

With their impressive manner, they will sway multitudes. They will deceive crowds that will clamor after them. Their deceits will prove so effective and winsome that the true Children of God will almost fall for their deceptions. These false leaders will enjoy great popularity.

I have seen the reality of this in my lifetime. I have watched men and women practice their deceitfulness to huge crowds. In city after city, multitudes swarm their meetings with enthusiastic responses, following them like sheep to the slaughter. Their books climb the bestseller lists. Some have even formed international denominations. Without question, the warning of Christ applies to our day as well. We must heed it.

The False Prophets Come in the Name of Jesus
He said, *"Many shall come in my name, saying, I am Christ."* Matthew 24:5 Some will come who will claim to be Christ. Throughout history, many have made this claim. They take the name of Jesus for themselves, yet reject, deny, and denounce the Jesus presented to us in Scripture. Others will state that they come as the *messenger* of Jesus, declaring validity for their messages.

The Bible describes characteristics that only one person has fulfilled, Jesus. No one else has fulfilled all of the signs, prophecies, and predictions given to us in the Bible regarding the Messiah except the Jesus described for us in Scripture. Further, historians have recorded His life and have described Him exactly as the Bible described Him. Scriptures give us confirmation that Jesus satisfies all criteria. Anyone can assume the title of the King of Kings, but none fulfills the criteria except Jesus. Jesus as described for us in Scripture is the true Messiah.

We should believe on the Jesus presented in the Bible because of the proof of experience. Everywhere that men and women have proclaimed the gospel of Christ it has produced the same response, without regard to color, nationality, social standing, education, or wealth. People throughout history, who have called upon the name of Jesus as described in Scripture, have experienced the exact same life change, without variation or change, always, always, always. He alone is our Deliverer, our Savior.

Demonstrations of the Power of False Prophets

Jesus warned, *"There shall arise false Christs, and false prophets, and shall shew great signs and wonders..."* Matthew 24:24 What does Jesus mean by this description?

The word "great" holds two meanings. One of them describes quality, like a great meal, tasteful as well as healthful. Further, it means quantity, abundance. Thus, a great meal can include the quality of the food as well as the amount of the food. In like manner, counterfeit teachers will provide signs and wonders of high quality and abundance. They will not produce a trick or slight of hand, but many high quality demonstrations.

What does the word "signs" mean? It describes some unusual occurrence that transcends the common course of nature. These false christs will do magnificent things, beyond the ordinary. They will use those displays as evidence of their calling, saying, "I told you I was the Christ. I told you I was from Jesus, and I had his message. Look what I have done."

Not only will they have these attesting signs but wonders, too. Wonders speak of the miraculous. A false Church leader may have the ability to perform miraculous and supernatural things. Some false leaders will exhibit astounding manifestations and claim a special anointing of God upon them.

Now, you can see how they are able to sway many people to follow them. No wonder many will conclude, "This Christian leader coming in the name of Jesus is so good, so clever. The messages we hear are often about Jesus. We see wonderful miracles that could only be of God. This person must assuredly be a prophet of God whom we can admire and follow."

Moses gave us a description of this very thing in Deuteronomy, thirteen centuries before Jesus birth, long before this dreadful error arose. Moses described this exact occurrence to help us know how to make the distinction. How can we discern the difference between the false and the true, the true messenger of God and the false messenger of God? They sound alike, so how can we know?

Moses issued this warning: *"If there arise among you a prophet, or a dreamer of dreams, and giveth thee a sign or a wonder, and the sign or the wonder come to pass..."* Deuteronomy 13:1-3

Then Moses delivered a discerning moment. If along with the sign and the wonder and that (s)he performs, if (s)he also says, *"Let us go after other gods,"* do not follow that one, because (s)he is a false prophet.

Note the point that Moses makes here. When someone comes in the name of Jesus and instructs to you to follow his/her teachings, examine not only the supernatural demonstrations, but the actual teachings of this person. Do the teachings lead you to Christ? Does (s)he develop the doctrinal truths of Scripture and point out to you what the Bible says? Does (s)he give another gospel, something not presented in Scripture?

Isaiah the prophet counseled God's people on this issue, too. He said, *"And when they shall say unto you, Seek unto them that have familiar spirits, and unto wizards that peep, and that mutter: should not a people seek unto their God? for the living to the dead?"* Isaiah 8:19 Then Isaiah described how to evaluate these circumstances: *"To the law and to the testimony."* Isaiah 8:20

When he mentions the law and the testimony, he means the Scriptures, referred to as the law and the testimony in that day. In essence, Isaiah instructed the people of God to go to the Scriptures. *"If they (the false prophets) speak not according to this word, it is because there is no light in them."* Isaiah 8.20

The word of God is the final authority. Take the message proclaimed by the attractive Christian leaders of our day and evaluate whether it agrees with Scripture. What do they say about the gospel? Frequently, their interpretation of the gospel identifies the first point of error with the following deviation: They reject the cross, they reject salvation through Christ alone, they reject salvation through his blood, and they reject the payment of blood of Jesus for the penalty of sin for people like you and me. Many offer a means of salvation outside the authority of Scripture.

Jesus loved His disciples, and He gave to them a warning, *"Take heed that nobody deceive you. For many shall come to you with my name saying, 'I am Christ.'"* They shall come in the name of Jesus saying, "I am the messenger of Christ. I am His prophet, His apostle, and His teacher. Observe what I can do and see that I am and anointed messenger of God. Follow me."

The Church today needs to heed this message of Jesus. False prophets, pastors, and teachers abound, and they influence multitudes with their deceits and apparent confirmations from God. The evil one uses them to divide and destroy the Church. With increasing faith in the Word of God, the followers of Christ must regard His warnings. We need to seek the guidance of the Holy Spirit to discern the false from the true, so that we may again experience God's glorious manifest presence in our lives.

Thank You, Lord Jesus, for giving us this lesson and preserving for us these instructions that You gave to Your disciples hundreds of years ago. They still apply to us today, and they serve to warn us that we might discern that which is false from that which is truth. Open our eyes, Holy Spirit, to see the true and the living Christ as revealed to us in the Scriptures. We ask You, Spirit of God, to bring that forth into our lives for I pray these things in the name of Jesus Christ, the Son of the living God. Amen.

Chapter Eleven

False Prophets: They Penetrate the Church in Disguise

"Jude, the servant of Jesus Christ, and brother of James, to them that are sanctified by God the Father, and preserved in Jesus Christ, and called: Mercy unto you, and peace, and love, be multiplied. Beloved, when I gave all diligence to write unto you of the common salvation, it was needful for me to write unto you, and exhort you that ye should earnestly contend for the faith which was once delivered unto the saints. For there are certain men crept in unawares, who were before of old ordained to this condemnation, ungodly men, turning the grace of our God into lasciviousness, and denying the only Lord God, and our Lord Jesus Christ." Jude 1:1-4

Wolves in Sheep's Clothing

Jude wrote this letter out of great concern for his brothers and sisters in Christ. When he recognized that false teachers had penetrated the Church under the guise of following Christ, he was alarmed. They were not true followers of Christ, but came to destroy His true followers. In his warning, Jude described several characteristics of these false believers who came to disrupt the Church. His explanations provide guidance to us in our quest to ferret out the errant Christian leaders in our day.

Depravity of Conduct

Jude described their depravity of conduct in verse 4, *"...certain men crept in unawares."* The hypocrisy of these false teachers gave them the appearance of true followers of Christ, but their behavior was deceitful. They hid their deepest thoughts, because they behaved like true believers, with clever words and actions.

Throughout history, men and women have followed this pattern. Many people claim to have made a "decision for Christ" at some time in their lives, but the experience produced only a temporary feeling and did not form a life changing choice. Others have made no choice at all. They have simply assumed the role of a Christian, thinking that one becomes a Christian by behaving like one. Some come as messengers of the evil one intent upon destruction of the Church. All of these various types of "Christians" inhabit the Church, even possessing positions of leadership. Jude's concerns are suitable for our day as well as his.

Wolves in Sheep's Clothing

Jude called these hypocrites ungodly men. Not only did they behave in a false manner, they also perverted the grace of God. In verse 4, Jude said that they had turned the grace of God into lasciviousness. In verse 7, Jude further described the wickedness of these who lived after the satisfaction of their own lusts. He said that they copied those who lived in *"...Sodom and Gomorrha, and the cities about them in like manner, giving themselves over to fornication, and going after strange flesh, are set forth for an example, suffering the vengeance of eternal fire. Likewise also these filthy dreamers defile the flesh"* Jude 1:7-8

These false men lived to satisfy their own fleshly desires and used their positions of influence and of authority to subvert and entice the unsuspecting. In Jude's day, false teachers crept into the Church and said, "Because of God's grace and His goodness, He has saved me. Therefore, I can live any way I want to live."

In our day, many people give the impression that they follow Christ yet pursue a lascivious lifestyle. They say, "I am free in Christ." By that, they mean this. "Since I have made a decision for Christ, I can do anything I want and live any lifestyle I choose. No one can criticize my behavior, because I have made a decision for Christ. One day I will inherit eternal life. Once saved, always saved. I am free in Christ."

The Bible does not teach that fallacy. The Scriptures teach that when you become a follower of Christ, you become a servant. Your lifestyle changes, and you become increasingly more like Christ. Jesus did not live His life according to His own will. He lived after the pattern, dictates, and commands of His heavenly Father. He lived a holy, just life. He commands those who truly trust Him to live holy lives, too.

Therefore, if we follow Christ, we cannot live any way that we please. Those who trust Christ do not have the freedom to live selfish, licentious, lascivious lifestyles. They cannot pursue the gratification of their own fleshly lusts and desires.

Though written hundreds of years ago, Jude's description of weakness in the Church depicts conditions prevalent in the Church today. Many pastors and Church leaders proclaim the same false message and live self-seeking lifestyles. They mislead unknowing multitudes into a condition of false security and hypocrisy. Jude's warning rings true today. The depravity of the conduct of these ungodly men led them to deny Christ. They claimed to follow Christ, but by their deportment they rejected Him. Their actions betrayed their speech. They denied His authority over their lives. You cannot claim to follow Christ and reject His authority over your life at the same time. If Christ is not Lord of all, He is not Lord at all.

Many untrustworthy teachers today separate salvation from lordship. They preach that someone can come to faith in Christ and, at a subsequent date or perhaps not at all, come to recognize Jesus as Lord. Yet, Jesus never separated these issues. Christ's disciples must deny themselves and submit to His lordship. Jesus rejects all others. (See Matthew 16.24-25.)

Disrespect for Authority

Not only did these deceptive leaders reject the Lordship of Christ, they spurned authority, thus becoming a law unto themselves. Today, many false leaders in the Church follow the same practice. They do not submit to any authority in the Church, either within a local Church or from other Church leaders. Some hold a virtual dictatorial position in their Churches.

This resistance affects their response to government. Peter and John faced a dilemma with government edicts, as did the four captives in Babylon. Their examples remind us to stand for God's commands when governments demand that we obey them instead of God. On occasions of direct conflict between man's law and God's law, we must submit and follow God's law. However, Paul in Romans 13 admonishes believers to obey government and give respect to government officials.

It is not unusual for false leaders to refuse to submit to government. They have become a law unto themselves. Frequently, it concerns restrictions on lavish lifestyles. The pursuit of money has blinded their eyes so that they have lost control of their behavior. It saddens me to see prominent Church leaders hide behind the Church to reject legitimate government authority. Jude warned centuries ago that disrespect for authority marks a false teacher. We should heed his counsel.

Deficiency of Knowledge

Jude identified another characteristic of faulty leadership, a deficiency of knowledge. He explained it this way, "*But these speak evil of those things which they know not: but what they know naturally, as brute beasts, in those things they corrupt themselves.*" Jude 1:10 They have never learned the truths of God, so they try to explain scripture without knowledge.

Jude called these men nothing more than brute beasts. They merely followed their natural instincts and behaved in ways that seemed normal and natural to their humanness in the same way that animals live by the nature that God has created within them. Therefore, they spoke falsely. Not knowing God, they spoke evil of things that they did not understand. They did not see things from God's perspective nor understand His will and ways.

Sadly, we experience a dearth of leaders who know God. You cannot know God by osmosis. You cannot know God unless you spend time with Him in study of His word and in prayer, conversing with Him. Praise God, there are a few men and women in positions of leadership who know God and spend time with Him. They stand in stark contrast to the many who try to represent the God they do not know.

Jude gave a warning. He said, these men creep in unawares. Do not follow them or listen to them. They talk about things they do not really understand, because they do not know God. They call good evil and evil good, because they really do not know the truth. (See Jude 1:11.)

Wolves in Sheep's Clothing

We need leaders who know God and are students of His word. They do not give a brief lecture on the goodness of man or a few steps on how to cure emotional ills. They tell you something about God and what they have come to know about God by experience. They encourage their listeners to pursue after God in intimate fellowship with Him.

Destitute of Character

Finally, in a series of pictures, Jude described these false teachers as destitute of character. He gave a lengthy list of characteristics to illustrate their destitution. These vivid descriptions explain their lack of character. He started in verse 11, *"Woe unto them! for they have gone in the way of Cain, and ran greedily after the error of Balaam for reward, and perished in the gainsaying of Core."* Jude 1:11

These three men carried out notorious acts. Cain killed his brother. Balaam attempted to prophesy against the Israelites as they traversed the wilderness toward the Promised Land. He did give counsel to Israel's enemies on how to lead God's people into immorality, which succeeded. Korah attempted to overthrow Moses, God's chosen leader of Israel. God judged him by causing the earth to open up and swallow Korah and his followers alive.

Jude described another character flaw, *"These [people] are spots in your feasts of charity."* Jude 1:12 They came to Israel's feasts, boldly appearing like Godly men. The literal meaning of this portion portrays them like rocks hidden under the water. They posed a danger to God's people, because, without shame, these hypocrites waited for the opportunity to cause believers to slip as if on rocks hidden under water. Jude warned his friends of that danger.

Jude used yet another picture to illustrate the worthless character of these false teachers. He said, *"They are like clouds without water."* Jude 1:12 What good is a cloud without life-giving, refreshing water? It is worthless. That explains the true worth of the false leaders. He also depicted their worthless character by calling them trees without fruit. Obviously, a fruit tree without fruit is valueless and succumbs to the axe.

In yet another way, Jude represented their lack of Biblical direction and stability by two pictures in verse 13. He called them "*Raging waves of the sea.*" The waves of the sea move in response to the wind. They move in whatever direction that the wind blows. The strength and direction of the wind determines the ferocity of the waves. In like manner, these leaders formed their messages and direction upon the whims of man.

He continued in verse 13 by describing them as wandering stars. Stars have a fixed path. Here, Jude made use of a Biblical type of using stars for leaders. However, these stars wandered, following no fixed path. Thus, God's people could not follow them, because the leaders did not know their direction, leading the flock one way this time and different way another time. Jude's friends could not rely upon their leadership.

He closed his denunciation of their character in verses 16-19. He called them *"…murmurers, complainers, walking after their own lusts; and their mouth speaketh great swelling words, having men's persons in admiration because of advantage... mockers walking after their own ungodly lusts...not having the Spirit."*

Jude categorized the false leaders of his day as hypocrites, worthless, and ungodly. His lengthy list of the poverty of character of corrupt leadership sadly applies to sinful practices today. Men and women that fit these same descriptions are elevated to positions of authority and responsibility.

Jude gave his warning out of love and concern for his friends and for God's honor. As he exhorted his fellow followers of Christ, I too, urge you with this warning. Do not follow those whose character and practices coincide with these warnings. Do not listen to them, do not buy their books, do not watch them on television, nor subscribe to their magazines and newsletters. They will not lead you to God, because they do not honor and exalt the Lord Jesus in their own lives.

I pray that the Spirit of God will open your eyes to see the truth of God's Word as revealed in Jude's warning to his friends. God has provided it for your protection. He loves His own, those who know God and have trusted Christ Who cares for them like a shepherd cares for his sheep. Heed these warnings from Scripture. Listen to the Spirit of God Who would instruct you to see and identify the false and to follow the true. I pray the Spirit of God will do that for you and lead you to fullness of joy, the rightful possession of the children of God.

Thank You, heavenly Father, for Your great love for us, which You have demonstrated in so many ways. You have preserved this letter from Jude to his friends warning them of false prophets and urging them not to follow them, with clear descriptions of what they would look like and how they would act.

Father, that description fits our day as well. I ask You to send forth Your Holy Spirit to us to open our eyes to identify false prophets, to turn from them, and to seek after that which is true. Help us to recognize the true messengers whom You have sent so that we might learn from them, come to know and trust You more fully, and to experience that joy and peace that is ours in Christ because we are Your children. We will give You thanks, praise, and honor, Father, Son and Holy Spirit, for what You accomplish. Amen.

Chapter Twelve

Essential Orthodoxy

"Take heed therefore unto yourselves, and to all the flock, over the which the Holy Ghost hath made you overseers, to feed the Church of God, which he hath purchased with his own blood. For I know this, that after my departing shall grievous wolves enter in among you, not sparing the flock. Also of your own selves shall men arise, speaking perverse things, to draw away disciples after them. Therefore watch." Acts 20:28-31

This passage is a description of the Apostle Paul's final meeting with the Church leaders from Ephesus. Paul had established a Church in Ephesus and appointed spiritual leaders in the Church. He met with them as he returned to Jerusalem, certain that persecutions awaited him. He wanted to give his friends some instruction about his future, even though it was somewhat obscure. His message combined a warning as well as directions on how to face the coming problems. He warned them that grievous wolves would come into their Church and draw many aside.

Wolves in sheep's clothing have infiltrated the Church. They have twisted the Scriptures to their own benefit and, as a consequence, the Church has declined. We can draw upon Paul's counsel and warning for encouragement and direction.

In his message, Paul compared these Church leaders to shepherds. God had entrusted them with the responsibilities of shepherds over His flock, the Church. They had a duty to feed the people of God, not with physical food, but with spiritual food. God required these shepherds to protect their flocks from their enemies, who wanted to destroy them. Finally, God expected these spiritual leaders to give direction to their flock. Paul emphasized these obligations, because he knew that danger lay ahead and he made it clear that spiritual leaders are to be shepherds.

We live in perilous times. False leaders victimize the Church. Faulty leadership of our day attacks and undermines Biblical doctrines. They teach that doctrine is not essential to Christian life. Even more dangerous, they say that no one can really know the truth.

This study will examine briefly seven Biblical doctrines that serve as the foundation of our faith in Christ. It will outline what spiritual food is essential to the Church, what truths are inviolate, and what paths are required for growth and safety. We must defend these truths against preachers who proclaim otherwise, and prove themselves to be the grievous wolves against which Paul warned.

(1) <u>The doctrine of God, His person and works</u> is provided in Scriptures with a list of His attributes. God has existed from all eternity in three persons: Father, Son, and Holy Spirit. As the only true and living God, He sovereignly created and controls all things according to His plan and purposes. Through His appointed Judge, Jesus Christ His Son, He will pronounce justice upon all who fail to trust and obey His word as revealed in the Bible.

(2) <u>Scripture teaches the nature of Jesus Christ</u>. True shepherds of the Church must believe and defend the person and works of Jesus Christ, the Son of God. Without eradicating His deity, He took upon Himself human flesh, born of the virgin Mary. He became the God-man, God in the flesh, in Whom dwells all the fullness of the godhead bodily. His works could fill volumes describing His supernatural miracles. His greatest work came when He gave His life on the cross as atonement to God for the sins of people like you and me.

Everyone is born with a sinful nature from the moment of conception, which alienates and separates humanity from God. This sinful nature so thoroughly permeates mankind that it renders us completely helpless to satisfy God or to reconcile ourselves to Him. The Bible describes humanity as dead in trespasses and sins. However, God made provision to reconcile sinners back to Himself through His Son, Jesus Christ, whose death brought reconciliation between God and people like you and me.

Everyone who comes to God through Jesus Christ will find forgiveness and peace with God. Justification by faith in Christ alone provides salvation for all who believe. His resurrection on the third day after His death and His ascension into the Father's presence confirmed it.

(3) <u>Foundational Biblical doctrine includes the person and works of the Holy Spirit</u>, an equal member of the godhead. Unlike humanity, He does not have a physical form. Although a spirit, He possesses the attributes of a person. Even though He is deity, He inhabits the lives of believers and works in them. Jesus taught in John 14-16 many of the works of the Holy Spirit, Who empowers believers with His supernatural authority and ability to serve God, worship and glorify Christ, and walk in holiness. He molds our lives into the image of Christ.

We do not hear very much about the Holy Spirit in our day. We have grieved Him, and in that process, we have quenched His work among us.

(4) <u>We must hold dear the several doctrines of salvation</u>. Today, the phrase "born again" carries little meaning. Some Christian teachers have taught this truth incorrectly to the confusion of many. Multitudes of people have done exactly what

Wolves in Sheep's Clothing

Paul said would occur. These wolves in sheep's clothing have come to destroy people's faith, and to guide them away from Jesus, the only Savior of sinners.

For this reason, I will discuss briefly several important doctrines of salvation, which we must believe in order to follow the Scriptures faithfully.

For example, you cannot make yourself born again spiritually any more than you can physically. You had nothing to do with your physical birth, and you have nothing to do with your spiritual birth. You can do nothing to deserve it or prepare the way for it. Religious actions, though earnestly and faithfully performed, contribute nothing to your spiritual new birth. The Holy Spirit produces the new birth through an experience called regeneration. It is a sovereign, gracious gift from God to you by the work of the Holy Spirit in you.

Once the Holy Spirit regenerates a person, He produces certain changes in those whom He regenerates…always. He causes you to repent from your sins. You turn from them and no longer follow your sinful lifestyle. Furthermore, He makes you trust Christ and Christ alone for your salvation. When you trust Christ, you become justified before a holy and just God. As the Holy Spirit works in your life, He produces a desire to follow Christ and obey Him.

These short statements identify the basic doctrines of salvation. By no means do they describe the totality of these doctrines. Volumes of books describe them in detail. As you grow in faith in Christ, the fullness of salvation will stagger your mind. The miracle of regeneration includes the nature of God, Jesus, and the Holy Spirit, as well as what you become in Christ... literally a new creature.

(5) The Church needs to understand the doctrine of the Scriptures, the Bible. Down through history, the enemy of the souls of mankind has attempted to destroy the Bible. Governments outlawed it and religious leaders misused it. Elitists have mocked it as something you cannot trust. While they admit that it contains good moral teaching, they contend that it contains error and is nothing more than a good book, unworthy of trust for eternal salvation.

Despite these challenges, God's word endures. The Bible offers trustworthy evidence and revelation of God. The Holy Spirit moved upon human instruments to record faithfully God's inspired message to humanity. Because of its inspiration by God, it is authoritative for life and practice. It describes the nature of God and the responsibilities of humanity to Him. When you believe and obey it, the Holy Spirit brings into your experience the reality of the Bible's message as it presents it. It presents how you can know God and experience Him your daily life.

(6) <u>Shepherds of God's people must preach the doctrine of holiness</u>. Many people revolt at this doctrine because they personally fall short of God's demands, and do not want to think about it. As children of God and followers of Christ, we must become increasingly holy. Our lives should show development from the day that we first trusted Christ. As we have grown older physically and our lives have changed, so our spiritual lives should also show growth. As believers examine themselves today in contrast to when they first trusted Christ, they should see a difference in their life styles and their thinking. They will find that they have lost former desires and interests and they will experience a growth in holiness.

All believers in Christ experience spiritual growth. Not all grow at the same rate or in the same fashion. However, they become increasingly like Christ. Let me ask you a question. Can you honestly say that you have greater interest today in pursuing after God and obeying Him than when you first trusted Christ? You should see a difference as the Holy Spirit works in your life. You will not attain ultimate perfection, but you should grow and develop spiritually.

Complacent pastors today do not emphasize personal holiness. People in their congregations do not want to be reminded of their sins. They do not want to review their spiritual failures. However, Paul reminded his friends from Ephesus of their responsibilities as teachers and as leaders to feed and tend their sheep. That work involves corrective ministry as much as any other aspect.

(7) <u>Finally, we must look at the doctrine of the Church</u>. The Bible describes how the Church should function. It tells how to identify spiritual leaders and explains how those shepherds should function. It reveals what we should do when we encounter leaders who lead people astray from Biblical teaching. It identifies that the Church is the body of Christ, a living organism.

Unfortunately, the Church has developed into nothing more than a business organization, and it follows all the patterns of secular structures. There is nothing supernatural in the Church today. One can explain it all in terms of management and business styles.

The Church is not an organization nor should it function like one. We need to return to the Scriptures and examine them for what they say about the Church. It is a living, vital thing. Moreover, it is called the body of Christ. He is the King. He is in charge of it. We need to counsel with the King to find out how He wants His body to function.

Most Churches do not do that today. They disregard the kingship of Christ in these matters. When you hear Christian teachers counsel the people of God away from the Lordship of Christ in issues of the Church, they identify themselves as false leaders. As wolves in sheep's clothing, they pretend to follow Christ but in fact deny His authority as enemies of Christ.

These seven doctrines comprise the foundational truths essential to true biblical Christianity. The false pastors and Church leaders of today attack these truths, as Paul warned. They are here full force, and the Church reels under their evil influence. I pray that the Holy Spirit will open your eyes to see the truth of these doctrines, their necessity, and, unfortunately, their absence in today's Church. May He lead you to pursue the truth and to conform your life to it.

Thank You, heavenly Father, for these wondrous truths that we have examined in a brief fashion. They outline the truth as presented in your Word about Yourself and the things You want us to believe and to defend. When we examine others about us who teach things contrary to these truths, may You open our eyes to see their errors, to turn aside from them, and to pursue the truth. I ask You, Holy Spirit of God, to open our eyes to understand the truths that we have examined, to believe them, and to commit our lives to them. May the belief of these truths ultimately bring a change in the way we live and act as we conform our lives to the truth. We will give to You, Father, Son, and Holy Spirit honor, glory, and praise for all that You accomplish. I ask these things in the name of Jesus Christ. Amen.

Chapter Thirteen

At Ease in Zion

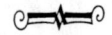

"Woe to them that are at ease in Zion, and trust in the mountain of Samaria, which are named chief of the nations, to whom the house of Israel came!" Amos 6:1

After the death of King David, the kingdom split into two, Israel to the north, Judah to the south. Israel had its king, Jeroboam II, while Judah's king was Uzziah. Amos served God as a prophet in Israel and Judah. In addition to his role as prophet, he was a shepherd and sheep breeder.

Amos' prophecy came at a time when both Israel and Judah had rebelled and rejected God. They maintained a formal appearance of worshipping God, while continuing to worship idols. Their simultaneous worship of both idols and God resulted in denial of Jehovah God, Who will not share His glory.

They further pursued after materialism. If you read a little bit further in this chapter, you read about the wealthy who lounged at their tables and in cots of ivory. They amassed great and sumptuous possessions and found pleasure and security in the abundance of things.

In an attempt to reach these self-satisfied people, God sent Amos the prophet to them with this message: *"Woe to you who are at ease in Zion."* Zion, another name for Jerusalem, served as the chief city of Judah. As an evidence of God's grace, He sent Amos to startle them and awaken them out of their false sense of contentment.

This passage is a serious warning to us, because false leaders of our day fail to teach the people to pursue God just as they did in the days of Amos. This Scripture reveals God's attitude toward sin. Though His warning proved His grace and mercy toward those who rejected Him, it also revealed His desire bring them back to fellowship with Him. The severity of the warning should prod us to examine our circumstances, because we, too, have many possessions and live self-satisfied lives. Faulty leadership of our day has lulled us to sleep with their mantra that "all is well in the Church."

The Church must recognize its true condition and heed the message that God gave to Amos thousands of years ago. We will identify, in the message of Amos, symptoms that relate to us, warning signs that will help us to turn from reliance upon uncertain things to pursue after God and the firm foundation that He offers. This text describes three symptoms of the conditions in the time of Amos, which describe the Church today.

They Rested on Inferior Peace

Notice the prophet's description: *"You are at ease."* The people enjoyed a safe and luxurious life with an abundance of material possessions. They did not fear attack from enemies for they were secure. Their life of ease gave them confidence that they needed nothing.

However, a strict definition of this word "ease" gives a better picture of their true condition. It literally means recklessness, carelessness. Therefore, in the midst of their prosperity with goods and possessions, there was a careless attitude about them. They lacked concern over the things, which should have concerned them. They enjoyed a manufactured peace, endorsed by the misleading messages of the evil prophets.

In similar fashion, the Church enjoys a smug contentment. We take pride in our "goodness." We live in peace and prosperity. We take pride in our works of charity, money we give to the poor. With few exceptions, we confront no severe conflicts. We applaud each other about religious accomplishments.

Our self-righteous contentment has degenerated into apathy. Church leaders plead desperately for people to serve in various positions, but their pleas are often unheeded. We fail to pursue God, preferring possessions. We create entertainments and productions for our enjoyment. These productions give us a certain happiness but divert us from the role of servants who will care for one another in the Body of Christ.

Remember that contentment and apathy do not necessarily translate into peace. As in the days of

Amos, one can rest on something thought to be firm and safe, only to discover its fragile weakness, and it crumbles. Big productions can produce a certain degree of happiness. Yet, when the programs end, and the lights go down, nothing has changed. The people who visited our Church buildings experienced a false joy.

We seem to have turned from God, the only source of true joy and peace. We neglect to pursue God. The counterfeit leaders of our day have led us to trade His manifest presence for a poor imitation.

I remind you of another prophet, Jeremiah, who gave the same message in his day that Amos did. In Jeremiah 6, as he spoke of the leaders in charge in his nation. Through His prophet God told the false prophets, kings, and elders, *"You have healed the hurts of your people only slightly. And you say 'Peace, peace' and there is no peace."* Jeremiah 6:14

Jeremiah and Amos spoke the same message: *"Woe to you, woe unto you who are at ease in Zion."* Their message rings true today. We cannot rest on our laurels. The spiritual condition of the Church is sinking. By the leadings of evil leaders, we have trusted in an inferior peace.

They Relied On an Imitation Power

The northern kingdom, Israel, trusted in the mountain of Samaria, which served as the headquarters of Israel. They worshiped God on that mountain and were secure as long as they held possession of it. However, if you read further in Amos' prophecy, you would discover that the enemy came in and took possession of the mountain of Samaria. Their mountain provided no safety for them in their time of need.

In similar fashion, the southern kingdom, Judah, trusted in the safety of Zion, or Jerusalem. The thick walls surrounding it with only 12 entrance gates made them feel secure. There came a day, however, when their enemy destroyed those walls, broke through the doors, captured Jerusalem, and laid waste to them. Their walls provided no protection to them in their time of need.

Notice that Amos commented about those named the chief of the nations, to whom the house of Israel is come. These people were the aristocracy, the leaders, and the elders. This broad group also included the kings and patriarchs of Israel and Judah. In each of their histories, God had blessed them greatly with men of God, like Abraham, Isaac, Jacob, and Moses. They had a wonderful heritage to pass on to their children.

Both kingdoms rested on this heritage. They thought that because of their past godly leaders they were immune to existing and future problems. They placed their confidence in their history, not in God. In Amos' day, they had a degenerate leadership, which neither followed God nor pursued Him. They sought false prophets and listened to them. Their incorrect hopes and reliance on their heroes did not succeed in the time of hardship.

Unfortunately, the Church today also relies on imitation powers. We have our heroes, too. We can identify past preachers and leaders whom God used mightily, but they cannot help us now. We need leaders and preachers today who will proclaim the truth and resist the enemy, regardless of consequences. The prevalence of counterfeit teachers today yields to society. They pacify the crowds and make league with the world in a vain attempt to create peace and security.

We look at our big mega-churches with their huge programs and think that we have arrived at a measure of perfection. We honor some of our leaders within the Church who have great influence in the world, but they are leading the Church down a path to destruction, because they do not seek the counsel of God.

In addition, we place great hope in apologetics, the defense of the gospel against attack. We follow leaders with dynamic presentations, but these forceful men cause us to rely upon man and not God. Our hope does not rest on good arguments. Our hope rests on God Who, by His Holy Spirit, overcomes attacks on the truth and convinces unbelievers of the truth when proclaimed.

We also use gimmicks to build the Church. Instead of earnestly seeking God's direction to build the body of Christ, advertising and promotion have become staples of the failing Church. Shallow leaders point to the excitement of their meetings and the expressions of emotion as evidence of the presence of God. This deceit leads to further decline in the Church.

Many present day preachers dilute the pure gospel of Christ by leaving out crucial elements and presenting part for the whole. In the hope that the world will find their message appealing, these misleading pastors give messages filled with generalities. They do not call their people to repentance or knowledge of grace that saves sinners. Thousands of people believe they have joined the redeemed of the Lord simply because they want to go to heaven and not to hell. They do not realize the full demands of a holy God. We are impressed by vast numbers of people who profess to be Christians but cannot sing the song of the redeemed, because they do not believe the saving truth of the gospel of Jesus Christ.

All of these examples reveal reliance upon an imitation power. Though results look attractive, they do not rest on God and the power of the Holy Spirit. They rely upon shaky foundations producing unsupported results. We must remember what God said to Zechariah, when he faced a difficult time. Later in his life, Jerusalem lay in ruins, and Zechariah began to rebuild it. From a human standpoint, Zechariah faced an insurmountable task. God assured him with this promise, *"It is not by might, nor by power, but by my Spirit saith the Lord."* Zechariah 4:6

We need, once again, to restore in our day the dignity of the Holy Spirit. We have set Him aside and refused to listen to His voice. Consequently, we have relied upon an imitation power. That described the day of Amos.

They Intentionally Rebelled against God

The false prophets and priests of Amos' day deliberately opposed God. The spiritual failure of the people came as a direct result of their evil leadership.

They mixed the insincere worship of God with the worship of idols made of wood and stone by their own hands, complete with sacrifices and the celebration of feast days. This man-made worship comfortably mixed with their natural cravings and pursuit of materialism. Their pluralistic worship made God only one among many Gods.

Let me just mention a few circumstances of the present-day Church that parallel people in the days of Amos. We have rampant sin in our day, even within the professing Church. Immorality exists, but worse than that, we see amorality, no morality. We have lost touch with the sacred. Pastors, preachers, and leaders fail to tell us the truth. They preach soothing messages that encourage us to think that everything is peaceful and good. They do not encourage us to examine ourselves in the light of God's word to see if we obey His demands upon us. We have a false sense of security in that we say in the casual recitation, "Once saved, always saved."

A false sense of security in a falsely presented gospel has led many to believe that they do not need to make any changes in their lives. Some rely upon a misleading view of freedom in Christ, which permits them to live as they please. Similar to the day of Amos, we have rebelled against God willfully. False leaders fail to encourage believers to pursue God alone.

The Church today replays the conditions of Amos' day, fostered by untrustworthy teachers. We rest on unsupported peace and an imitation power, because we have rebelled against God with willfulness.

Just before they stoned Stephen as described in Acts, he told them that they resembled their past leaders. He said, *"You always resist the Holy Spirit. You refuse to follow God."* Acts 7:51

Paul in his letters warned of a similar sin: *"Don't grieve the Holy Spirit."* Ephesians 4:30 In his letter to the Church at Thessalonica, he said, *"Don't quench the Holy Spirit."* 1 Thessalonians 5:19

The words of Stephen and Paul echo what happened in Amos' day and in ours. By resisting the Holy Spirit, we have thrown cold water on His works and extinguished His fires. We have offended Him with our sinful rebellion. As a result, we have a false sense of peace and power.

If it is wrong to call the works of the Holy Spirit the works of men (and it is), it is equally sinful to call the works of men the works of the Holy Spirit. That describes our trouble. We identify the works of men as the works of the Holy Spirit. To experience once again the glorious manifest presence of God by His Holy Spirit, we must repent of our sin and return to the pursuit of God.

I call on the Church to heed these warnings in the book of Amos and realize that we stand on the brink of judgment. We must examine to see whether we have substituted ease, contentment, and imitation power for the true peace of God. We must restore, once again, the dignity of the person of the Holy Spirit of God.

Heavenly Father, thank You for this record that You have given to us through Your man of God thousands of years ago, Amos, who called his people to pursue after You and to forsake that which is false. I pray that You will use these same warnings in our day to cause us to awaken to the true circumstances where we live, to turn from them, to repent from them, and to pursue after You. Help us to forsake our sin and to forsake those false leaders and prophets who would lead us astray. Enable us to seek after the truth of your Word so that we might rest upon true strength and power. Grant that we might experience the reality of Your peace. We will give You, Father, Son and Holy Spirit, honor, glory, and praise for what You accomplish in our lives. I ask these things, Father, in the name of Jesus Your Son. Amen.

Chapter Fourteen

Christ Centered Preaching

"For after that in the wisdom of God the world by wisdom knew not God, it pleased God by the foolishness of preaching to save them that believe. For the Jews require a sign, and the Greeks seek after wisdom: But we preach Christ crucified, unto the Jews a stumblingblock, and unto the Greeks foolishness; But unto them which are called, both Jews and Greeks, Christ the power of God, and the wisdom of God." 1 Corinthians 1:21-24

After Paul's presentation on Mars Hill in Athens, he went to Corinth to proclaim Christ to its citizens. Located on the Grecian coastline near the Aegean Sea, Corinth had become a major city in Greece at the time of Paul. Because of its great commerce, the people of Corinth had wealth and affluence. Along with their desire for money and possessions came rampant sexual immorality. As he spoke in Corinth, many people came to trust Christ as Lord and Savior, and, in his first letter back to them, he reminded them of the centrality of Jesus Christ and the cross.

This setting pictures our land today, a land of wealth, affluence, and a lusting for possessions of all kinds. In addition, sexual promiscuity and immorality pervade our land. It has become accepted practice. We very much mirror the city of Corinth. As Paul reminded his friends at Corinth of the importance and the centrality of Jesus Christ and the cross, so we in our day need to remember that only Christ and the cross can provide for us what we need for life, Christ and the cross. The message has not changed nor has the need changed. We need today what Paul's friends in Corinth needed thousands of years ago.

The Jews wanted a sign from Christ as proof of His claims as Messiah. They wanted Jesus to do some supernatural sign for them that would convince them of His veracity. When Jesus refused to comply with their demands, the Jews rejected Him. Because of the Greeks' pursuit of wisdom, they wanted the gospel presented in a scholarly way. When Paul presented the cross of Christ, which seemed foolish to them, they rejected the gospel.

In our day people have much the same reaction to the cross and to the preaching of Jesus Christ. Many demand visible signs to convince them of the truth of the gospel. To others, it appears foolish. Our society emulates Corinth.

As an antidote to this spiritual poverty, the Apostle Paul proclaimed a Christ-centered message. The false prophets and teachers of Paul's day agreed with the Corinthian culture. They rejected his Christ-centered message for one that was more appealing socially. It sounds familiar, doesn't it? False Christian leaders in our day follow the same path as those in Paul's day.

In this text, Paul outlined the essentials of Christ-centered preaching. In this message to his friends, Paul explained three marks of Christ-centered preaching. We will examine them so that we can understand this all-important emphasis. Then, we can identify and reject those false prophets and leaders who fail to provide it, and search for those who preach Christ.

The Church experiences a dearth of Christ-centered preaching today. Many profess to preach Christ in spite of their failure to do so. Before we examine the marks of this ministry, I want to identify several confusing fallacies. For example, expository preaching in and of itself does not necessarily qualify as Christ-centered preaching. I have heard many "expositions" of Scripture that never mentioned Christ.

Many preachers emphasize evangelism of the lost. In this fashion, they believe that they preach Christ. However, as mentioned in earlier chapters, many leave out crucial elements of the gospel. They present part of the gospel as the whole of the gospel. Thus, they do not present the gospel of Christ accurately.

Further, some false pastors and leaders feel that if they read from the gospels as part of the Church service, that qualifies as presenting Christ. Merely reading about Christ's actions does not provide a Christ-centered ministry.

Many current leaders teach only the ethics of Christian living. They urge their listeners to follow the example of Jesus and live a selfless life as He did. Emulation does not qualify as possession. In some ways, you can act like Jesus and never know Him. Although it might lead to a life of high quality, it will not necessarily lead you to saving faith in Jesus, the Savior of sinners, like you and me.

Not one of these preaching methods meets the criteria of Christ-centered preaching. Although these errors may provide some glimpses of Jesus and His life and even encourage us to emulate Him, they do not fulfill the requirements of what God has called us to do. The Bible reveals Christ as the only way to God. He has called us to worship, obey, and trust Christ. Christ-centered preaching teaches us how to do that.

The Depravity of Man

Christ-centered preaching presents the depravity of man. Many pastors fail to present the sinfulness of man. They skirt the issue. In fact, many of them will say, "We don't talk about sin in our Church or in our materials." These leaders openly admit that the subject of sin is not a part of their "ministry."

I remember a time when I heard a preacher give a message on a text that contained a very definite list of "dos and don'ts." Surprisingly, he completely avoided those sections of his text. After the service, I approached him with a question. "How come in your message you didn't talk about the parts where it said 'don't do this…avoid this and this?'"

He immediately responded, "I only preach a positive message. I don't talk about anything negative."

Wolves in Sheep's Clothing

That mindset permeates many in our day who profess to speak for God and lead the Church. They completely avoid the discussion of sin. That does not fulfill Christ-centered preaching.

Christ-centered preaching emphasizes and proclaims the depravity of man. Because Adam and Eve sinned in the Garden of Eden, sin has entered into the nature of humanity. Every one of us has a sinful nature from the moment of conception. That cute little child or grandchild that you hold in your arms possesses a sinful nature, which *"...(is) estranged from the womb: they go astray as soon as they be born..."*

Every child has a heart of rebellion and disobedience. The Scriptures say it this way. *"Foolishness is bound in the heart of a child."* Proverbs 22:15 We do not like to view children that way. However, as soon as they have the opportunity, children will divert their will and attention away from God.

We are sinners not because we sin - we sin because we are sinners. That is the bent of our heart. We willfully, deliberately pursue a life away from God, because of our sinful natures. A Christ-centered ministry will present that truth and point out other candid features of our nature as human beings.

Our sinful nature makes us totally helpless in any pursuit after God. By nature, we neither like nor love God. We are hopelessly dead in our trespasses and sins, as the Scriptures describe us; we do not want to pursue Him. We cannot meet the demands of a holy God. We not only lack the ability to satisfy God, we also lack any desire to meet His commands.

A Christ-centered ministry presents these truths mentioned in Paul's text. In verse 21, he talked about how in the wisdom of this world man did not desire after God. He reminded his friends what he had taught them, when he preached to them initially. He proclaimed to them their depravity before God.

Jesus preached this same truth in His conversation with Nicodemus. Christ said, *"He that believeth on [Christ] is not condemned: but he that believeth not is condemned already."* John 3:18 In other words, as sinful men and women without Christ, we stand before God condemned, justly deserving the just wrath of God upon us. Further in that same conversation with Nicodemus, Jesus said, *"He that believeth on the Son hath everlasting life: and he that believeth not the Son shall not see life; but the wrath of God abideth on him."* John 3:36

Christ-centered preaching presents the depravity of man and points out to men and to women their lostness before God. They stand before God condemned, incapable of any good, incapable of any kind of correction, incapable of any kind of righteous living that would satisfy God. In our day we need a return to true Christ-centered preaching that proclaims the depravity of man.

Deliverance from Sin through Faith in Jesus Christ Alone

Many preachers of our day (that I would call false prophets) do not present Jesus as the only Savior. They present salvation in a variety of ways. For example, many of them in our day say that every religion has its "Jesus." They teach that those who have the Bible, have the Jesus described in it; other lands and cultures have someone like Jesus that they follow. Thus, many "Jesuses" exist. They teach that it does not matter which Jesus you follow as long as you follow and believe one of them. In error, they call it Christ-centered preaching.

Furthermore, these same teachers and preachers completely avoid the cross. I recently researched a very prominent young preacher of our day. He travels around the world, preaches to multiplied thousands who come to his meetings. The world proclaims him as one of the young, dynamic preachers of our era. With occasional vague references, He does not preach the cross.

No salvation exists for sinners like you and me without the cross. Any message of salvation presented to you as a passageway into eternal life with God that does not include the cross will not save you. You will ultimately discover that you still stand before God condemned.

Paul mentioned to his friends and reminded them, "The preaching of the cross calls to men and women to believe and to faith in Christ."

Unbelievers have said, "Why do we need to hear about the cross and all that blood? Jesus did not die on the cross. He just swooned, and His followers took him down from the cross. They hid Him away and later said he came back to life. We don't believe any of that."

Why must we believe what Jesus did on the cross? We need a brief reminder of Jesus' great accomplishment on the cross and of what He fulfilled. On the cross, He presented Himself to God as a substitutionary sacrifice as payment in full for the penalty for sin on behalf of men and women like you and me. When He offered Himself on the cross, He gave His life there. He did not swoon on the cross. He shed his blood, His body was broken, and He died there. God the Father looked down on His sacrifice and accepted it. Christ's death on the cross fulfilled a payment in satisfaction to God the Father on behalf of people like you and me.

That explains why God accepts only those who come to Him through Christ. (See John 14.6 and 1 Timothy 2.5.) When a sinner comes to God, (s)he must come through faith in the Substitute, Jesus Christ.

I remind you that a Christ-centered ministry preaches deliverance from sin through faith in Jesus Christ alone. We cannot contribute anything to our salvation, because of our inherited sinful nature and the substitutionary sacrifice of Christ for sinners. Therefore, sinners receive salvation through faith in Jesus Christ as their substitute, alone, with nothing else added to it. Christ-centered preaching presents Jesus Christ as the satisfaction for the sin of people. Any other preaching will not reconcile you to God.

Thus, when we have faith in Christ, we enjoy benefits that accrue to us. We experience freedom from guilt. We enjoy freedom from the foolishness of endless self-analysis. We possess freedom from endless self-preoccupation. A profound prominent mark of false teaching today is the emphasis upon "**me**ism." This preaching stresses maximizing of yourself and reaching your full potential, with all of your emotions and your psychologies blended correctly to produce a full emotional you.

These teachers do not even talk of Jesus or of God. They fail to talk about what Jesus fulfilled and accomplished on the cross and what it will provide in our lives when we fully trust Him. Yet without Christ-centered preaching that proclaims deliverance from our sinful human natures, souls will not be saved. Paul said, *"We preach Christ crucified."* 1 Corinthians 1:23 Those who believe in Christ alone will find salvation through His blood.

The Demands and Delights of the Life of Christ

We tend to view salvation as a one-time experience. We believe that some day in the future we will inherit eternal life. We act as though our salvation in Christ has no bearing upon our everyday life. We live as we have always lived, pursuing our own dreams and desires. We disregard anything in between the time when we trusted Christ and the time when we will enter into eternal life as if it has no bearing on our lives.

That is a commonly held fallacy. Christ makes demands upon those who of us who trust Him and have claimed His payment on the cross for our sins to the satisfaction of God the Father. For example, He said, *"Unless you deny yourself, take up your cross and follow me, you are not my disciple."* He taught His disciples how He expected them to live. He has made demands upon all who trust Him, which He commands us to obey. The Scriptures describe the pattern of life of Christ's followers.

Following Christ brings delights, too. Christians have barely scratched the surface of fully understanding the effect that faith in Christ can have upon their lives. Faith in Christ brings fullness of joy, freedom, peace, and security to our minds and hearts because of Jesus and what He accomplished and fulfilled on the cross. Full realization of its fullness requires that believers present themselves daily to Jesus, asking Him to bring into our lives that which He provided for us in His life, death, resurrection, and ascension to the right hand of the Father.

John described in his first epistle how his friends could have fullness of joy in Christ. What Christ accomplished on the cross has a bearing upon every aspect of our lives. It makes no difference whether we are married or single, rich or poor. It has an influence upon our family life. It has a bearing upon how we work. It affects our friendships, as well as our choices in life regarding our time, our talents, and our treasures.

The false prophets, teachers, and leaders of today reject all of these aspects of Christ-centered ministry. They reject the depravity of man, deliverance through faith in Christ alone, and fail to present the demands and delights of Christ upon our lives.

Whom do you follow? Whose preaching do you admire? What books do you read? What television programs do you watch? What radio programs capture your time? If they do not provide Christ-centered teaching and preaching, you follow false prophets and false teachings. Their teachings will not encourage you to walk with Christ; no, they will not lead you to fullness in Christ, and they will lead you astray.

What we have just examined from the Scriptures may not have meaning to some of you. It may sound strange, because you have never trusted Him. His teachings have no meaning to you or affect upon your life. To you, I urge you to call upon you to trust Christ. Call upon Him now.

Jesus said, *"Come unto me, all ye that labour and are heavy laden, and I will give you rest."* Matthew 11:28

Jesus said, *"I am the way, the truth, and the life: no man cometh unto the Father, but by me."* John 14:6

Jesus said, *"..and Him that cometh to me I will in no wise cast out."* John 6:37

I pray that the Spirit of God will open your eyes to see your need of trusting Jesus and that He will bring about in you that faith and trust in Jesus, the only provision for sinners.

To those of us who have trusted in Christ, I ask that you realize what it means to have a Christ-centered ministry. False messengers and their false messages bombard us. They look and sound good, and they appeal to us. Nevertheless, their false messages will lead us astray. We need to have truth upon which we can rely so that we can discern between the true and the false. We must reject the false and not toy with it. We must not imagine that we can experiment with false teaching, because it will eat away at the spiritual foundation on which we build. It is important to discern between the true and the false in order to place ourselves under Christ-centered preaching that will build in us a strong faith.

I pray that the Spirit of God will help you to have that foundation upon which you can rest. It will help you discern the true from the false, so that you might experience fullness of joy in Christ.

Thank You, heavenly Father, for Your provision for us in Jesus Christ. Thank You for what He accomplished in His life, His death on the cross, His resurrection, and His ascension to sit at Your right hand in the glory of heaven. Thank you for Your grace and for Your mercy.

Father, I ask that You would send Your Holy Spirit to bring into our daily lives faith in Christ to the saving of our souls. Please bring into our lives the fruit, the benefits, the blessings, and the delights of what Christ accomplished for us. May they permeate our daily experience and all of the affairs and activities of our lives that we might enjoy that which He has provided for us. We will give to You, Father, Son and Holy Spirit praise, honor, glory, and thanks for what You accomplish in our lives. I ask these things in the name of Jesus Christ Your Son. Amen.

Chapter Fifteen

Spiritual Effectiveness: Communication by the Spirit

"And I, brethren, when I came to you, came not with excellency of speech or of wisdom, declaring unto you the testimony of God. For I determined not to know any thing among you, save Jesus Christ, and him crucified. And I was with you in weakness, and in fear, and in much trembling. And my speech and my preaching was not with enticing words of man's wisdom, but in demonstration of the Spirit and of power: That your faith should not stand in the wisdom of men, but in the power of God." 1 Corinthians 2:1-5

As we previously observed, Corinth possessed three characteristics, wealth, wickedness, and wisdom. Because they prided themselves in their heritage and ability to discern great truth, they expected that of others.

In this passage, Paul described the first time he spoke of Christ to the Corinthians. He reminded them that he did not come in the fashion to which they were accustomed. He certainly could have, because he studied under the greatest teachers of the Scriptures of his day. A well-educated and highly trained man, he could have relied upon his brilliance in the Scriptures.

However, Paul described his entrance this way, *"When I came to you the first time I came to you in great weakness, fear and trembling."* He wanted them to realize an important issue: the contrast between the way that the world presents wisdom and the way that God presents it. This text identifies the difference.

This description provides important lessons for us. Solomon wrote, *"There is nothing new under the sun."* Ecclesiastes 1:9 Mankind is still governed by money, wantonness, and wisdom, as were Paul's friends at Corinth. In many ways, our nation and the professing Church fit the description of Corinth. Therefore, we are not surprised that preachers of today follow the pattern of the world in their appeals to us. We have adopted culturally influenced means and methods of presenting the gospel as well.

This example from Paul's life also enables us to see how God presents the truth concerning Himself. We have great misunderstandings of Biblical truth, because we approach it as we approach every other kind of knowledge. We "study" God and His provision in Christ the same way that we "study" science, mathematics, business, or literature. The unique nature of God requires that His Holy Spirit must enlighten our minds to understand spiritual truth. The examination of Paul's approach to the Corinthians helps us to distinguish between false and true ways in which to present the gospel.

Paul distilled this passage into two criteria for true ministers and teachers of the gospel of Christ. They reject the culture's means of understanding truth and they rely on the Holy Spirit to reveal truth. They accept the scriptural admonition that fulfilling God's plan for the Church requires faith in God, not man. Paul's testimony contrasts starkly with the methods of today.

Apologetics

Paul said that he did not come to Corinth with excellence of speech nor enticing words. This admission revealed that he did not follow the communication method of that day. Corinthians took pride in the compilation of works they created which outlined methods of persuasion. Current orators referred to this set of books to determine their method of teaching, and they were considered highly successful. Paul did not follow the pattern of the orators of his day.

Some Christian leaders teach by a similar method of apologetics, using skillful argumentation in an attempt to defend the gospel. Although teaching through apologetics may prove the rationality of the Scriptures, it has not proven to be an effective means of revival in the Church and the world. When Paul presented Christ, he spoke with simplicity and the power of the Holy Spirit.

Endorsement

Another modern day means of presenting the gospel of Jesus is endorsement. Some bring famous figures of our day to give their support to Christ. They often call on newly converted popular personalities, sports figures, and popular entertainers to "prove" the acceptability of the gospel message.

Polls

A further example of the world's methods used in the Church is the trust given to polls to direct Church plans. Poll results determine sermon topics, program selection, types of meetings, even music. Demographic studies sometimes dictate location and create congregation targets for the income and racial makeup of the Church.

Presentation

The presentation of the gospel with programs designed to appeal to human nature and to attract multitudes has become very popular. Holiday events for Easter, Christmas, or political rallies draw crowds. The productions concentrate on vivid, colorful tableaus that appeal to the senses, engender a warm feeling, but lack the power of Christ. Many pastors tend to confuse the spectacular with the supernatural. However, a spectacular presentation designed to appeal to human nature does not guarantee the supernatural power of God. The supernatural can be spectacular, but the spectacular is not necessarily supernatural.

We feature music groups and bands to stir excitement and enthusiasm and call it the moving of the

Holy Spirit. We appear to confuse emotion and excitement for the Holy Spirit. Certainly, the work of the Holy Spirit affects people's emotions; but it cannot be manufactured. The mere presence of emotion and excitement does not equate to the presence of the Spirit. Though crowds may come, they leave with a false gospel in their ears and emptiness in their hearts.

Appeasement

Teachers and preachers who do not want to offend anyone employ a method of appeasement. These teachers design their messages in terms that will make their audiences feel good about themselves. They fail to preach the demands of holiness that Christ requires of those who follow Him.

We can explain almost everything about today's Church in terms of means and methods. In many churches apologetics, endorsement, polls, presentation, or appeasement have become the authoritative voices that dictate plans. As a result, the Church pays no attention to God's Word, giving the people what they want, instead of what they need. The Church has rejected Paul's counsel and chosen to concentrate upon the world's ABCs of Church growth, attendance, buildings, and cash. These techniques contradict Paul's method of proclaiming Christ to Corinth.

What do we mean when we talk about the demonstration of the Spirit and of power? I suggest a few evidences of the power of the Holy Spirit.

Ordinary People Become Saints

The Holy Spirit turns sinful, wicked men and women into saints, which describes believers in Christ. Their lives demonstrate it. The demonstration of the Spirit and of power will produce true, Biblical saints who do not have to refer to the Greek original to prove it.

The Gospel is Preached with Divine Power

The demonstration of the Spirit and of power anoints a preacher with unction. Unction, a Biblical term, describes one totally absorbed by God. The preacher with unction speaks with a fervency and urgency, which consumes the speaker. The preacher is on fire, spiritually speaking.

Weak and ineffective preachers do not speak with the unction of the Holy Spirit. They may deliver messages based upon some Scripture reference or Biblical theme. However, they lack the power of the Holy Spirit in their preaching.

The Spirit of God Invades the Meeting

The power of the Holy Spirit affects the atmosphere of the meeting. I do not refer to the air that you breathe, but to the sense of God's presence. Awe pervades the place. Without anyone asking for silence, a spirit of quiet reflects holy conditions that occur supernaturally, without manipulation. People are gripped by a holy fear, for God has invaded the meeting and made Himself known to those present.

Wolves in Sheep's Clothing

Supernatural Activity is Sometimes Visible

Many in leadership positions in professing churches reject supernatural activity. They say, "That is not for our time in history. These things are not for us." In this way, the Church has completely shut off a whole function of the Spirit of God, Who alone can produce supernatural activity. Many in our churches need God to work in a supernatural way in their lives but never seek it, because their leaders tell them not to pursue the supernatural, miraculous work of the Spirit of God.

Let me suggest to you some ways in which we need to have the supernatural activity of God in our day. For example, everyone's salvation results from a supernatural act. You cannot save yourself; it comes from a supernatural work of the Holy Spirit in a person's life. Nor can a believer grow in Christ into holiness without the Spirit's power.

In addition, prayer depends upon the supernatural intervention of God relative to the request. It is clear that a direct correlation exists between the rejection of the Spirit's supernatural work and the decline in prayer. Despite the hundreds of promises in the Bible for answered prayer, believers simply do not believe that God answers prayer. Prayerlessness thus pervades the Church today. Prayer and faith in the supernatural work of God by His Spirit go hand in hand.

Perhaps you have heard of Jim Cymbala, pastor of the Brooklyn Tabernacle in Brooklyn, New York. When he arrived at the Church he now pastors, only a handful of people attended. He set aside one night a week, Tuesday night, only for prayer. He invited the people to bring their prayer needs and requests to the meeting, where those that gathered would spend time in prayer. When they began to pray, God heard their cries and answered, supernaturally. I have heard Pastor Cybala report that more people now attend the Tuesday night prayer meeting than the other regularly scheduled meetings, because they believe that God answers prayer.

Unfortunately, many Church leaders explain away the obvious. The Church must turn to God in prayer to plead for mercy from Him to intervene again, supernaturally. Prayer can be and should be a vital relationship between you and God, where you bring to Him your needs, and you expect Him to answer. God still answers prayer.

I have pondered the question as to why we do not see miracles in our day. Many people say it is because God no longer performs miracles. However, I am a prime example that God works miracles today, because I can tell you what God has done for me. I will give you one example. Following surgery to remove a medically confirmed tumor, the doctor approached my wife and shaking his head exclaimed, "I can't explain it. It is not there. It was there on the operating table before surgery, but it is gone without one single evidence of infection." God still performs supernatural miracles in our day. He has for me several times.

I admit I do not know why He does not do more, though one reason surely comes from the fact that we do not ask. We fail to ask Him to perform for us those things that only He can do. We must ask Him to do something no one else can do – a miracle.

The things that we just examined illustrate what Paul means when he said, *"When I came to you, I came to you in demonstrate of the Spirit and of power."* Certainly, there is more. The Holy Spirit worked in Paul beyond human explanation. The Corinthians saw it and believed Paul's messages. In similar fashion today, we need to see once again the supernatural working of the Holy Spirit, not the explainable ways so often presented to us today.

Where has the Spirit of God identified in your heart and life a failure to apply these truths? Do you rely upon the ways, means, and methods of the world to try to understand God? Do you follow those who choose the world's ways instead of reliance upon the Holy Spirit?

I pray that the Holy Spirit will open your eyes to see the abundant supernatural works that He can and will provide to His children who ask Him. He waits for your call.

Dear heavenly Father, thank You for this vivid example we have from Your servant Paul. It shows us how You used him, and how he relied upon You by Your Holy Spirit to demonstrate to the Corinthians the truth and reality of Yourself. Father, I pray that in Your grace and mercy by Your Holy Spirit You will demonstrate the truth and reality of what we have examined, especially concerning the Lord Jesus Your Son. Open our eyes to understand the truth, that we might commit our lives to it, trusting Your Son Jesus exclusively as Lord and Savior, and that we might be reconciled to You through His blood. We will give You thanks, Father, for what You accomplish. I ask these things in Jesus' name, Amen.

Chapter Sixteen

Where Do We Go From Here?

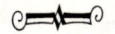

"Beloved, when I gave all diligence to write unto you of the common salvation, it was needful for me to write unto you, and exhort you that ye should earnestly contend for the faith which was once delivered unto the saints. For there are certain men crept in unawares, who were before of old ordained to this condemnation, ungodly men, turning the grace of our God into lasciviousness, and denying the only Lord God, and our Lord Jesus Christ. Jude 3-4 But ye, beloved, building up yourselves on your most holy faith, praying in the Holy Ghost, Keep yourselves in the love of God, looking for the mercy of our Lord Jesus Christ unto eternal life. And of some have compassion, making a difference: And others save with fear, pulling them out of the fire; hating even the garment spotted by the flesh." Jude 20-23

We have examined the ways to discern false prophets by reviewing Scripture's description of their characteristics. We learned how to identify them, not only by the ways they behave, but also by the errors they teach, and the truths they fail to teach. This final study examines how the Scriptures instruct us to respond to false prophets and teachers.

In this passage, Jude told his friends how followers of Christ should respond to false leaders. These believers became aware of ungodly men who had crept in among them, teaching false doctrines, and leading many astray. Jude felt compelled by the Spirit of God to say, "Stop! We must identify these misleading teachers and properly respond to them."

The warning he gave to his friends in that first century fits our day, because we also face false prophets. They proclaim their false messages on television, on radio, and in their books, which proclaim faulty doctrines and false hopes. We need Jude's warnings and direction on how to react to them. Believers must recognize them for their own security and well-being as followers of Christ. They must separate from false leaders who would lead them astray from the truth. These teachers mock the name of Christ and declare a false image of God and His truth.

Now that we have some discernment from Scripture regarding false prophets, where do we go from here? Jude outlined in the letter to his friends three steps for followers of Christ to take in response to ungodly leaders.

Contend for the Faith

Jude exhorted his friends to contend for the faith. What did he mean when he told them to "contend?" That word comes from the sport of gymnastics, an active event in Jude's day. It describes the contest among competitors who strive for a prize. Each of them wants to win the victory wreath and wear the crown. They contend with all their concentration and energy.

Contending for the faith includes overcoming faulty notions. We must have a knowledge and understanding of the truth to identify error. It calls for examination of those whom we follow in order to discern between the false and the true. (1 John 4.1-3) We do not follow them just because they come professing the name of Jesus. We must examine them and test them to see if they teach and obey the truth.

Jude urged the Church to fight and struggle with all their strength against false leaders. He cried to them to ward off the adversary with fervency and zeal.

That flies in the face of much of what the professing Church proposes today. At this point, fallacies arise that prevent many from resisting error. Many call it unChristian to fight for the truth. Yet, Jesus gave us a clear example when He fought against the scribes and Pharisees of His day. He spoke against their false teachings with strong derision. (Read Matthew 23, for example.) Jesus always pointed out error as He spoke the truth.

Many in our day fear what people will think, when they stand for the truth. They suspect they will be chastised for causing division and splits in the Church and will be seen unfavorably by their friends.

Sadly, we spend a lot of time contemplating what other people will think of us. We use it as an excuse for inactivity and failure to obey God. We sacrifice the truth for the sake of false unity in order to avoid hurt feelings. That is compromise.

Another fallacy rests upon a wrong interpretation of "judging." Many misinterpret Jesus' statement from Matthew 7.1, "*Judge not lest you be judged*," as meaning that Christians should not judge anyone at all. In fact, if you read the rest of the chapter, you will notice that Jesus did not tell His audience not to judge. He instructed them on *how* to judge. He warned that they would suffer judgment in the same fashion that they judged others. Therefore, judge with care. Make discerning, careful judgments based upon Scripture and the truth. We dare not let error grow because of a misunderstanding about judging.

Others deflect the counsel of Jude by thinking that it does not matter, or is unimportant. The spiritual welfare of the Church matters. It reflects on the glorious name of Christ and His honor. If it does not matter, why did Jesus pray the Father to send the Spirit of Truth to believers? Why, did He call Him the spirit of Truth? He prayed the Father to send the Holy Spirit for this very reason: the truth matters. Believers need the Holy Spirit to guide them into the truth.

Many believers think that the teachings of false prophets and teachers do not affect them. Untrustworthy doctrine does influence how we live. It causes doubt and unbelief, which are enemies to faith in Christ. It generates questions about God and

His character. All of these weaken individuals and the Church.

The last fallacy is the toughest one of all, because it sounds so spiritual. This error causes many to say, "I'll stay here, and I will stand for the truth. Even though the leadership of the Church possesses the characteristics of false prophets, I will stay here and try to fix it." It is wrong to think that you can stay and fix error in the Church. In 1 Corinthians 15.33, it says, *"Be not deceived: evil communications corrupt good manners."* When Paul spoke of evil communications, he described companionships, friendships, and relationships. He reminded his friends of the dire consequences of evil associations that corrupt their good habits, character, and moralities. Sin never improves upward.

With sorrow, I tell you that you will not fix error in the Church. Scripture confirms this conclusion. Jesus, for example, never stayed where the people did not want Him. In fact, when He sent out His disciples on a mission and gave them power of all kinds of evil things, He told them what to do if the people rejected their message. He said, "If you go into a city or into a house and they reject you, leave. Shake the dust off your feet. Go to the next town."

One of the hardest things for people to do is to leave a church. You have friends there. You have happy memories associated with that church. You may know the pastor and his family very well, and you care about them. You have a level of comfort in this fellowship.

Wolves in Sheep's Clothing

However, if the pastor and the church's leadership exhibit the features of false prophets, you face a difficult decision. If you determine that they do not proclaim the truth nor follow scriptural directions, you must not stay there. Paul warned his friends, *"Come out from among them and be ye separate."*

What I am calling on you to do is not easy, but it is the right thing to do. Jesus did not tell us it would be easy to be His disciple. In fact, He called it a cross. He said, "If you want to be my disciple, take up your cross and follow me." That is what God calls us to do. A dear friend of mine put it in a memorable statement. He said, "If you run with a skunk, you will smell like one." Unfortunately, you will not fix the erring Church.

My friends, this is no time for games. We are to stand for the truth. Jude wrote his friends, "I have written to you to urge you, because of the false men that have come in amongst you," he said, *"I have written to you that you earnestly contend for the faith."*

The Bible records Paul's confrontation with Peter, when Peter behaved incorrectly in the church. To Peter's credit, He heeded Paul's admonition. (See Galatians 2.11-16.) Again, Paul warned his beloved Timothy of false prophets and told him not to follow or listen to them. (See 2 Timothy 2.16-18.)

Once we identify the false prophets and teachers, we must reject them. In both the Old and New Testament, the Scriptures give us that directive. God's word commands us to avoid and withdraw from them. It warns us not to listen to them or their teachings, even if they perform miracles that appear from

God. (See Deuteronomy 13.1-4, Jeremiah 23.14-22, 1 Timothy 6.1-5, and 2 Timothy 3.1-5.)

A final aspect of contending for the truth requires that we seek God and find leaders who seek God. As when Samuel went to look for the man after God's heart, we must avoid looking at the personality and appearance of someone. Depend upon the Holy Spirit to help you see the heart. The heart expresses itself in outward behavior. A Godly man or woman will exhibit Godly character.

Conform to the Truth

In verse 20 of his short letter Jude said, *"But ye, beloved, building up yourselves, building up yourselves."* Jude 1:20. He further told then, *"Build up yourselves on your holy faith. Pray in the Holy Ghost. Keep yourselves in the love of God looking for the mercy of our Lord Jesus Christ unto eternal life."* Jude 1:20-21 Experience God yourself and confirm it. Know that it is true and then conform your life to it. Live after that truth. Conform your life to the truth.

The advice of Jude parallels Paul's advice to Timothy. Paul told him, "Hold fast to the truth. Do not trade it for that which is false. Hold to the truth."

"Till I come, give attendance to reading, to exhortation, to doctrine. Neglect not the gift that is in thee, which was given thee by prophecy, with the laying on of the hands of the presbytery. Meditate upon these things; give thyself wholly to them; that thy profiting

may appear to all. Take heed unto thyself, and unto the doctrine; continue in them: for in doing this thou shalt both save thyself, and them that hear thee. 1 Timothy 4:13-15

Paul advised Timothy about a crucial issue that we see in our day among deceitful leaders; the love of money. Jesus warned of this when He said, "You can't serve two masters. You can't love both money and Me at the same time." This issue permeates the Church today among many who profess to come in Christ's name. They boast of their wealth, they wear costly designer clothes, and boast of their jets and palatial homes,

Paul warned Timothy of this very evil, *"The love of money is the root of all evil."* I Timothy 6:10 He added this further admonition, *"While some coveted after, they have erred from the faith, and pierced themselves through with many sorrows. But thou, O man of God...Flee those things ...* I Timothy 6:10-12 Flee from them. Turn from them. *Follow after righteousness, godliness, faith, love patience, meekness. Fight the good fight of faith.* "Contend for the faith whereunto you are called." 1 Timothy 6:10-11

Conduct Yourselves with Compassion

"And of some have compassion." Jude 1:22 Paul spoke to the believers when he said, "Have some compassion. In your withdrawal and deliverance from doubters, have some compassion. Deliver some so as by fire, dragging them out. Do not stay there with them, but drag them out." Jude desired compas-

sionate confrontation, not contentious confrontation. He wanted his friends to stand for the truth, but to speak the truth in love.

These comments are confirmed in chapters two and three of the book of Revelation. This passage contains seven letters dictated to John by the Lord Jesus, which John delivered to the appropriate churches during his lifetime.

If you read those two chapters, you will discover that error, sin, faithlessness, and demonic worship consumed six out of seven. These Churches followed false gods, even permitting false teachers to teach. You will find that in every instance Jesus rebuked them. Jesus does not smile at unbelief, which deeply offends Him. Through John, the Lord Jesus rebuked these churches for their sin. He chastised them and called them to repentance. He instructed the members of the churches, "Turn aside from the false teachers and follow Me." God rebukes unbelief every time at every turn, among those whom He loves, such as Peter.

I pray that by now you perceive the severity of the problem. This is not merely a difference of opinion. This is a pervasive, severe problem. The professing Church today contains false prophets, pastors, teachers, and leaders who lead it into dangerous confusion and unbelief.

I trust that you see the attitude of God toward it. God is deeply displeased. He is righteous, and He will withhold His favor from a Church that is casual about truth. There will be no blessing, and He will judge.

Scripture is consistent in its teaching that God does not tolerate sin. Repeatedly He judged His people when they turned away from Him and embraced sin. Beginning with His dealing with the Children of Israel described in the Old Testament, His believers depicted in the New Testament, and in the Church throughout history, God's judgment is sure.

One of the first and most severe judgments is His withdrawal. Because it happens subtly, we often do not realize it. Gradually, we begin to replace the actual presence of God with man-made enthusiasm. We may clap and sing, "Praise God!" but He withholds His blessing. God never blesses that which is false. He may permit it. He may even allow it to have some kinds of beneficial results to its followers, but that is not His blessing.

Read the vivid example in the Old Testament where the Children of Israel cried, "God, give us meat. You have given us this manna, and You have given us water, but can You provide meat?" God said, "How much meat do you want?" So, he sent them quail. Do you have any notion how much quail God sent to those Children of Israel? The quail that God sent covered a circle 32-40 miles across, 3 feet deep. My friends, that is a lot of quail! (Numbers 11.31-35)

They were so thrilled that thousands of them literally gorged themselves to death eating that quail. We read the writer of Psalms harking back to that instance. David wrote, *"God sent them quail because they asked for it."* But, here is the part I want to impress upon you. *"But he sent leanness to their souls.*" You call that a blessing? That is a judgment. (Psalm 106.15)

The greatest judgment they suffered was not death by gorging themselves on the quail. They experienced leanness of their souls because God was not there.

The same condition describes the Church today. We cannot address the issues that I have expressed in these studies on our own. We need the Holy Spirit. We need the Spirit of God first to teach us the truth so that we know the truth and we need Him to give us discernment so that we can distinguish between the false and the true. Admittedly, sometimes the line is pretty close and hard to discern. How will we do that? The Spirit of God, the Spirit of Truth, will guide us into the truth. Remember. Jesus said, *"And I will pray the Father, and he shall give you another Comforter, that he may abide with you for ever; Even the Spirit of truth; whom the world cannot receive, because it seeth him not, neither knoweth him: but ye know him; for he dwelleth with you, and shall be in you."* John 14:16-17

The Church needs a revival. I do not mean an artificially generated experience with music, where the preacher jumps around and people fall on the floor as if swayed by the presence of the Holy Spirit. That cheap imitation does not come from God. I am talking about a revival where the Spirit of God moves and convicts of sin so profoundly that men fall on their faces before a holy God and cry out to Him for mercy. We must see our true condition before God. We cry out to Him for mercy, because He demands holy lives from His children. We need a revival that proclaims the truth that calls upon men and women to repent and turn from their sin, and to believe and trust Jesus

Will you respond? I pray that the Spirit of God will open your eyes to see the truth and to cause you to trust Him and to conform your life to the truth in faith.

Dear heavenly Father, You did not say it would be easy to follow You. However, You did tell us that You would never leave us or forsake us. You would be with us, You would help us, and You would give us strength. When we encounter difficulty, frustration, temptation, and trial, You promised You would help us. You promised You would comfort us, encourage us, and enable us by Your Holy Spirit to do that which You call us to do.

Father, I pray for my friends that in Your grace and mercy that You will send forth Your Holy Spirit to them to open their eyes to see the truth and to bring them to faith and trust in You. Bring about in them the spiritual revival that they need and that I need so we might be true followers of Christ, children of God who are different, who conform to the truth of Your Word, that Your name, Father, and the name of Jesus Your Son, would be honored, glorified, worshipped, adored, and feared. We will give You honor, glory and praise, triune God for what You accomplish. Amen.